HOW TO PLAY BRIDGE

(PT. 3)

PTARMIGAN BOOKS

HOW TO PLAY BRIDGE

by Hubert Phillips
and Terence Reese

PENGUIN BOOKS
LONDON and NEW YORK

First Published in 1945

MADE AND PRINTED IN GREAT BRITAIN
FOR PENGUIN BOOKS LTD., HARMONDSWORTH, MIDDLESEX,
BY HAZELL, WATSON AND VINEY, LTD., LONDON AND AYLESBURY.

CONTENTS

PART I. HOW THE GAME IS PLAYED

PART II. THE BIDDING

PART III. THE PLAY

FOREWORD

THE first three chapters of this book describe how Bridge is played, for the benefit of those who know nothing about it. They can be omitted by other readers. In arranging the rest of the book we have followed the usual practice of discussing bidding before play. But a complete beginner is likely to find bidding easier to understand if he has read the chapter on play first, proceeding from Part I to Part III.

Readers who have heard tell of the manifold "systems" and "conventions" used by Bridge players may be surprised by our lack of reference to such things. Although we have not stressed the point in the text, the style of bidding here described is, in fact, that of the Approach-Forcing system, universally known and played. As in our larger work, *The Elements of Contract*, we have concentrated on expounding the principles which must underlie all good Bridge, whatever the fashion of the moment.

Our object has been to give an outline of the game sufficient to enable a novice, unfamiliar with cards, to take a hand—with enjoyment to himself, and without giving offence to others—after one careful reading.

H. P.
J. T. R.

PART I. HOW THE GAME IS PLAYED

CHAPTER I

ABOUT TRICKS AND BIDDING

IF you have never played a game of the Whist family, you may know nothing about the ranking value of cards, so we will begin right at the beginning. You probably do know that in a pack there are 52 cards, 13 of each suit, Spades, Hearts, Diamonds, and Clubs. The cards rank in the following order:—Ace (the highest), King, Queen, Jack, Ten, Nine, Eight, Seven, Six, Five, Four, Three, Two. The meaning of rank becomes clear when we consider the play to a " trick." Imagine four players seated in positions North, South, East, and West. They will be dealt 13 cards each, and all play one card to each of 13 tricks.

Let us assume that for the first trick the West player leads and the cards played to the trick are :

These cards are played in clockwise order. First the Queen of Hearts by West, then the King by North, the Ace by East, and the five by South. The trick is won by East because he has played the highest-ranking card, the Ace. East and West are playing in partnership, so it is a trick won by their side.   As East has won this trick, it is up to him to lead to the next trick.

Now you will note that in this example all four cards were of the same suit.   That is in accordance with the invariable rule that whenever possible the players should follow with a card of the suit led.   Of course it must happen towards the end of a hand, and may happen at the beginning, that a player has no cards in his hand of the suit led.   Then he has to play a card of another suit, but except in special circumstances the card he plays has no power to win the trick.   So the play to a later trick might be :

In this example the first play or lead is made by East and is the Three of Diamonds.   South has no Diamonds and discards the Ten of Spades.   West follows with the Seven of Diamonds and North with the Six of Diamonds. Now although South's Ten is the highest card played, it has no power to win the trick because it was not of the suit led.   The trick is won by West's Seven of Diamonds.

THE FACTOR OF TRUMPS

There is one most important exception to the principle given in the last section, that a trick is won by the highest card of the suit led.   The exception arises from the fact that the majority of hands are played with one suit as "trumps."   This trump suit has paramount rank over all the other suits ; so that if Spades are trumps, the Two of Spades beats the Ace of any other suit.   Nevertheless, the rule that a player must follow suit if he can remains good. If Spades were trumps, the play to a trick might go:

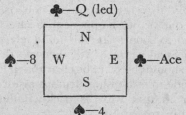

North leads the Queen of Clubs and East plays the Ace. If South has a Club, he must play one, but if he has not, he can trump, and he does so with the Four of Spades. West also would have to play a Club if he had one, but not having one, and having a higher trump than South, he can play it, over-trumping South's Four of Spades with the Eight of Spades and winning the trick.

The Bidding

What suit, if any, shall be trumps is determined by the bidding which precedes the play. At Whist the trump suit was established automatically by turning up a card. At an early form of Bridge the dealer could name trumps, but at Contract Bridge the two sides bid against one another to determine whether there shall be No-Trumps or what particular suit shall be Trumps. From the illustrations we have given of the power of the trump suit, it should be easy to understand that the side which has the majority of trumps has a big advantage in the business of trick winning. Suppose you pick up a hand like this:

♠—A K Q J 5 2
♡—K 6
♢—Q 7 3
♣—K 4

Now if Spades are trumps, it is almost certain that all your six Spades will win tricks, but if Hearts are trumps and the opponents hold most of them, your Spades are unlikely to win more than one or possibly two tricks, for one or other opponent is sure to be short of Spades and as soon as he has none left he will trump your good Spades which will thenceforth cease to win tricks. It should therefore be clear that it is to the advantage of a side to establish as trumps a suit in which it is strong, for in that way its trick-winning possibilities are greatly increased.

The Meaning of a Contract

It is understood, then, that the general object in the bidding is to select a favourable trump suit. But there is more in it than this. Every bid made is, in a way, a claim that if this bid is not contested by the opponents, the side which has made the bid will win a given number of tricks if the suit mentioned in the bid stands as trumps. For example, a player dealt the hand given above :

♠—A K Q J 5 2
♡—K 6
♢—Q 7 3
♣—K 4

would bid One Spade. This would mean that if nobody overcalled his bid, he would have to try to make, with the help of his partner's cards, the odd trick of the 13, with Spades as trumps. A call of One Spade is a contract to make seven of the 13 tricks, a call of Two Spades to make eight tricks, a call of Three Spades to make nine tricks, and so on, till you come to a call of Seven Spades which is called a Grand Slam and carries with it the ambitious promise to make all 13 tricks.

In practice it is unlikely to happen that this call of One Spade will go uncontested. After the dealer has made this call of One Spade, the player on his left has to make a call. He can either say " No Bid," or make a call which ranks higher than One Spade. There is a ranking order of suits which is as follows :—No-Trump, Spades, Hearts, Diamonds, Clubs. One Spade would overcall One Heart, and One No-Trump would overcall One Spade, but to overcall One Spade with another suit it is necessary to make a call at a higher range, for example Two Diamonds. If this call is in fact made by the second player, the third player (the partner of the opener) can either pass or make a call higher than Two Diamonds. In making his bid he will take into account the fact that his partner has already given certain indications of his holding by making the opening call of One Spade. So the bidding progresses until finally a call is made, perhaps Four Spades, which is passed by the next three players. Then the hand is played with Spades as trumps, and the player who has called Four Spades has contracted to make ten tricks out of 13 in the play. If he succeeds, he scores certain points, and if he fails, he loses points. This is the factor which limits the bidding between the two sides in their struggle to establish a favourable trump suit. If, in this instance, the opponents were to persist with their Diamond suit against Four Spades, they would have to call Five Diamonds, thereby undertaking to make eleven tricks. If they judged that this was far beyond their ability, it would not pay them to continue, for in addition to the calls so far described, there is another called " Double." When a player judges that his opponents have under-taken a contract which he is confident that they cannot fulfil, he can double, and if the double is left in, no further call being made, the scoring both for the enemy if they nevertheless succeed in making their contract, and for the doubling side if it defeats the contract, is greatly increased. Furthermore, a side which is doubled, if it expects to succeed in its contract can make the call of

" Redouble," thereby increasing the score yet again. These calls of Double and Redouble do not affect the range of the bidding in so far as overcalls are concerned. Thus, Four Hearts might be called by West, doubled by North, and redoubled by East; but South could then overcall with Four Spades, just as he could have overcalled an undoubled bid of Four Hearts.

DECLARER AND DUMMY

There is one point of primary importance in the playing of a hand which has not so far been discussed. The player who in the bidding is the first to mention the denomination, a suit or no-trumps, which becomes the final contract, becomes the " declarer," and in the play of the hand controls his partner's cards as well as his own. The bidding is, of course, conducted with all the hands held up. The opening lead is made by the player on the left of the declarer. The declarer's partner, known as " Dummy," then lays all his cards face upwards on the table, and Dummy's cards are thenceforth played by the declarer.

The dummy player is not allowed to make any suggestions or comments during the play of the hand. The only right he possesses by law is to draw attention to an irregularity, such as the gathering of a trick by the side which did not win it, or something of that kind. He is also allowed when his partner, the declarer, fails to follow suit, to ask him if he has none of the suit led, thus warning him against committing a revoke which involves serious penalties.

CHAPTER II

THE PLAY OF A COMPLETE HAND

THE last chapter gave some account of the elements of the game. It taught the ranking value of cards and suits, the meaning of tricks and trumps, the general purpose of the bidding, and the relation between declarer and dummy. In this chapter a full account is given of the procedure from the cut for partners to the end of the first hand.

PRELIMINARIES TO THE DEAL

When four players decide to make up a bridge game, the first thing they do is to cut for partners. A pack is spread out on the table and the four players withdraw one card each. When everyone has taken a card, they are turned up and the two players with the highest cards play against the other two. Suppose that the four cards cut are the Ace of Spades, the Nine of Hearts, the Nine of Diamonds, and the Six of Clubs ; the players with the first two are partners because the Ace is the highest card and of the two nines the Heart is higher because Hearts rank higher than Diamonds.

The player who has cut the Ace of Spades—the highest card—deals the first hand, and his side has choice of seats and cards, for it is usual, though not essential, to play with two packs of cards, which are used for alternate hands. Let us say that the dealer chooses to occupy the seat which we call South, and asks for the red cards. His left-hand opponent (West) shuffles the red pack and then puts it down on his right. The dealer then passes it across to his right-hand opponent (East), and on the way he can exercise his right to the last shuffle. East cuts the pack into two portions and South completes the cut by placing what was the lower half

of the pack on top of the rest. South then deals the
cards one by one, first to West, then to North, then to
East, and then to himself. The last card should fall to
him, and if it does not, then there must have been a mis-
deal, and the cards must be cut and dealt again.
During the deal, the other pack is taken in hand by the
dealer's partner (North), shuffled by him and placed
on his right.

When the deal has been completed, the players pick
up their cards and, the more readily to appraise their
character, sort them into suits. Let us suppose that
when this has been done the players survey these hands :

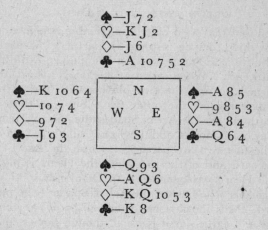

♠—J 7 2
♡—K J 2
◇—J 6
♣—A 10 7 5 2

♠—K 10 6 4
♡—10 7 4
◇—9 7 2
♣—J 9 3

N
W   E
S

♠—A 8 5
♡—9 8 5 3
◇—A 8 4
♣—Q 6 4

♠—Q 9 3
♡—A Q 6
◇—K Q 10 5 3
♣—K 8

As South dealt, he has to bid first. If he had a weak
hand, he would say " No Bid," but as a later chapter
will show, he has ample strength for an opening bid,
and would in fact bid One Diamond. West speaks next,
and having no sound call, he should pass. This is best
expressed by the words " No Bid." North then bids
his best suit, Clubs. As Diamonds rank higher than
Clubs, One Club would be insufficient, so North bids
Two Clubs. East passes, and South's best bid is now

Two No-Trumps. West passes and North raises his partner's call to Three No-Trumps, which everybody passes.

It is too early for the reader to appreciate the reasons for all this bidding, but it can be said at this point that in bidding to exactly Three No-Trumps, North-South have undertaken what is called a game contract. If they succeed in fulfilling this contract to win nine of the 13 tricks (for remember that a contract of Three involves a claim to make 6 + 3 tricks in the play), they secure a " game " which is worth a lot in the scoring, whereas a contract of Two No-Trumps would be worth much less. And if, say, Four No-Trumps were bid, an extra trick would have to be made for the fulfilment of the contract and no more would be scored than if Three No-Trumps had been bid and Four made.

THE OPENING LEAD

When everybody has passed the bid of Three No-Trumps the bidding is ended, and no further calls can be made. The declarer in this instance, the player who has to handle the dummy's cards in addition to his own, is South, because although North made the final bid of Three No-Trumps, the first bid in this denomination (No-Trumps) was made by South when he called Two No-Trumps on the second round. The opening lead is made by the player on the left of the declarer, in this case West. West's proper lead (the reasons for which we will discuss in a moment) is the Four of Spades. When this card has been placed on the table, North puts all his cards face upwards on the table, and thereafter must fulfil his designation of Dummy by refraining from taking any part whatsoever in the play of the hand, except that he is allowed to warn his partner, the declarer, against revoking, that is, failing to follow suit when he can do so.

THE PLAY

It is understood, then, that henceforth North's cards are played by the declarer, South. We suggest to the reader that in order to follow the play, he should lay out all the cards. This is how the play might go :

Triok 1. West leads ♠ 4, North plays ♠ 2, East plays ♠ A and South plays ♠ 3.

In leading from his longest suit, West is pursuing sound strategy in the defence to a No-Trump contract. He aims to drive out the high cards of the suit, so that later on he will be able to win tricks with low cards to which no one else can follow.

In playing the lowest Spade from dummy, South follows another sound general principle which is " second hand low." He could make an abortive attempt to win the trick by playing the Jack, but since in the Queen he holds an equally good card himself which he can play if it is needed to win the trick, it would be very misguided to play the Jack and give East the chance of felling this useful card with his Ace.

East, on the other hand, must play his top card, following another sound general principle, to wit, " third hand high." He could do no good by holding up his Ace. On the contrary, he should win the trick, so that he can play back the suit to his partner. After the Ace has been played, South naturally plays his lowest card. East having won the trick, West should gather the cards and place them face downwards in front of him. The trick is then said to be quitted, and thereafter no one may look at it. It is therefore necessary for all the players to pay attention to each card played, because later in the hand it may be vital for a player to know whether a low card of a suit is the best outstanding or not. Although the novice may find it difficult to believe, the effort of memory needed at bridge to know which cards of a suit have been played is extraordinarily slight. With a little practice even players of quite moderate ability find no difficulty in remembering what has gone. In fact, really one does not have to remember at all; as long as one sees the trick, that is enough to fix it in the mind of almost anyone.

Trick 2.   East leads ♠ 8, South plays ♠ 9, West plays ♠ 6, and North plays ♠ 7.

East can judge from West's opening lead of the low Spade that West has length in the suit, and as he has three to the Ace himself, and he can see three in the dummy, he can tell that in continuing this suit he is pursuing the most promising line of defence.   To return partner's lead is generally the right line of defence at No-Trumps.   In this case East has no alternative which is in the least attractive, for Clubs are held strongly by dummy, Diamonds have been bid by the declarer, and it will take a long time to make anything of East's length in Hearts.

The most interesting feature in the play to this trick is West's refusal to win it with his King.   He has a very good reason for this play.   It is that he places the Queen with South, and knows that he must lose at least one trick in the suit.   He hopes, however, that South and East have exactly three Spades each, so that his own long card in the suit will win the fourth trick.   In order to make this long card, it is necessary for him to obtain the lead after it has been established.   If he wins this second trick with the King and plays the Spade back, he will be left with the master card in the suit but he will never get in to make it.   Therefore he holds off this trick, with what effect will appear when we come to trick 4.   As declarer has won this trick, he gathers the cards and lays them in front of him.

Trick 3.   South leads ◇ 3, West plays ◇ 2, North plays ◇ J, and East plays the ◇ A.

South at once attacks the suit which, when developed, will bring him the most tricks.   Note that he does not play Hearts simply because he has the Ace King Queen of the suit.   To play these cards would not give South any extra tricks which he would not otherwise make. On the contrary, the sole effect would be to establish the long card in the suit which is held by East.   It would be equally bad to attack Clubs, for at best that would set up two tricks in addition to the Ace and King which can be made at any time.   But by the simple process of driving out the Ace of Diamonds, declarer can—unless the suit breaks 5-1, which is very unlikely—establish four tricks in the suit.   East has nothing to gain by holding up his Ace of Diamonds, and if he did South would continue to play the suit until the Ace was forced out.

This is the second trick won by the defence, and it is placed aslant the first, so that the tricks won by the side can be readily counted.

Trick 4.   East leads ♠ 5, South plays the ♠ Q, West plays the ♠ K, North plays the ♠ J.

Now we can appreciate the value of West's hold-up play on the second trick.   Had he played the King of Spades then and followed with another round, East would not have had a Spade to lead at this point and West would never have got in to make the thirteenth. Even if East could not be sure that his partner held the King, he should still continue the suit with a view to establishing the long card which his partner no doubt must hold.

Trick 5.   West plays the ♠ 10, North plays the ♣ 2, East plays the ◇ 4, South plays the ◇ 3.

As he has seen three rounds of the suit played to which everybody has followed, West knows that his last Spade is the master, even without reflecting that all cards higher than the Ten have been played.   Such a calculation very quickly becomes quite automatic.   The other players discard, as they cannot follow to the suit led.

We need not continue with the play in detail, for it is obvious that whatever West leads to the sixth trick, declarer can easily make all the remaining tricks. In fact, his position is so strong that on the fifth trick he has to throw away a winning Diamond. In actual play, South would probably expose his cards at this point, claiming the remainder, and after a quick glance the defenders would agree, and all the hands would be thrown in. The players then enter the score and proceed to the next deal.

You will remember that the second pack was shuffled (the word usually used is " made ") by North and placed on his right. It is therefore now on the left of West who will pass it across to South for the cut, and when this has been completed West will deal, the pack with which the first hand was played being made by East and placed on his right ready for the next dealer, North.

CHAPTER III

THE SCORING

IF you have not a proper bridge scorer, any rectangular strip of paper will do. Draw a line down the centre and another line across the middle. The score for your own side is written in the left-hand column and that of the opponents in the right. The reason for the line across the middle is that the scoring falls into two parts, above the line for penalties, honours, and bonuses, below the line for tricks. We will take the latter first.

SCORING BELOW THE LINE

It has been explained that a contract of, say, Four Spades involves a claim to win ten tricks. A side which

makes its contract of Four Spades scores below the line
$4 \times 30 = 120$, because Spades and Hearts (the major
suits) score 30 a trick. The minor suits (Diamonds and
Clubs) count 20 a trick, so that Three Diamonds, for
example, scores 60 below the line. At No-Trumps the
first trick counts 40 and all subsequent tricks 30 apiece.
When 100 points are scored below the line game has
been made, and when a side has won two games it has
won the rubber and the score is added up.

To score game from a love score it is necessary to make
Three No-Trumps $(40 + 30 + 30)$, Four Spades or
Hearts (4×30), and Five Diamonds or Clubs (5×20).
Game can, however, be made in separate stages. A
side might contract for Two Diamonds, for example, and
make it, the score of 40 being called a part score. To
make game now only 60 is needed, so that Two Hearts
would be enough. When a game is scored a line is
drawn beneath it, and a side which has scored a game
is said to be " vulnerable." The effect of that will be
understood when we come to the next section.

Scoring above the Line

Above the line are scored all points which do not con-
tribute to the making of game. These points consist of
penalties in respect of contracts not made, overtricks
made above the number contracted for, slam and rubber
bonuses, and honours for certain high card holdings.

Penalties for Undertricks. The score for penalties is as
follows, for a side which is not vulnerable :

undoubled—50 for each trick short of contract.
doubled—100 for the first trick ; 200 for subsequent
tricks.
redoubled—200 for the first trick ; 400 for subsequent
tricks.

Thus to be three down doubled not vulnerable
would cost 500 $(100 + 200 + 200)$. If the side which

fails to make its contract is vulnerable, the penalties are :

undoubled—100 for each trick short of contract.
doubled—200 for the first trick ; 300 for subsequent tricks.
redoubled—400 for the first trick ; 600 for subsequent tricks.

So three down doubled and vulnerable would cost 800 (200 + 300 + 300).

Scoring for Overtricks. When a side scores more tricks than it has contracted for, the overtricks score the usual amount of 20 or 30 a trick according to the contract. So if Two Hearts is bid and Four made in the play, the score is 60 below the line and 60 above for overtricks. It will not do to enter 120 below the line, because that would represent game, and having contracted for Two Hearts only, the side can score below the line the value of no more than Two Hearts. If Three No-Trumps is bid and Four made, the score should strictly be written 100 below the line and 30 above, but as game has been scored in any case, the figure 130 can be entered below the line without causing any upset.

If the contract has been doubled or redoubled, scoring for tricks is twice or four times the normal amount. Overtricks non-vulnerable are 100 a trick if doubled, 200 if redoubled ; and vulnerable 200 and 400 respectively. So if the bid is Four Hearts redoubled and Five is made, the score below the line is $4 \times 120 = 480$ and the overtrick would be 200 if non-vulnerable and 400 if vulnerable.

It is important to realise that a double of a part score may present the opponents with a game. If Two Spades is doubled and made, the score below the line is $2 \times 60 = 120$, enough for game.

Slam and Rubber Bonuses. There are special rewards for a side which successfully contracts for 12 tricks, a small slam, or 13 tricks, a grand slam. The bonus for a small slam is 500 non-vulnerable, 750 vulnerable ; for a grand slam 1,000 non-vulnerable, and 1,500 vulnerable. The side which wins the rubber, being the first to make two games, scores a bonus of 700 if the opponents have not made a game, and 500 if they have. For a side's first game no bonus is directly scored, but nevertheless it has an unseen value of rather more than 300, because it puts the side half-way towards winning the rubber.

Honours. If any player has four of the five honours (Ace King Queen Jack Ten) in the trump suit, he scores a bonus of 100, and if he has all five honours 150. If at No-Trumps he has all four Aces, he scores 150.

A Typical Rubber

We will end this chapter by setting out the score of a typical rubber. The contracts and results are given first, and the reader should compile a score sheet of his own and then compare it with ours.

1st Hand : Opponents play in Four Spades doubled, and are two down.

2nd Hand : We bid Two Clubs and make Four.

3rd Hand : Opponents bid Three Hearts and make Five.

4th Hand : We bid Three Diamonds and make it.

5th Hand : Opponents bid Two No-Trumps and are three down.

6th Hand : We play in Four Hearts redoubled and are one down.

(If you have scored correctly so far, you will realise that we are vulnerable.)

7th Hand : Opponents make an overtrick in Six Diamonds doubled and one of them has four honours.

8th Hand : Opponents are two down in Three Clubs doubled.

9th Hand : We bid Three No-Trumps and make Four, one of us having all four Aces.

This is how your score should read—the figures in brackets refer to the hand on which the score was made :

500 (9)	500 (7)
150 (9)	100 (7)
500 (8)	100 (7)
150 (5)	400 (6)
40 (2)	60 (3)
300 (1)	
40 (2)	90 (3)
60 (4)	
	240 (7)
130 (9)	
1,870	1,490

The difference is 380 in our favour, and counting to the nearest 100, as is usual when there are any stakes, you would say that we had won a rubber of four points.

❧

PART II. THE BIDDING

CHAPTER IV

VALUATION AND OPENING BIDS OF ONE

THERE are certain fixed standards for opening bids, and the purpose of this chapter is to teach a player how to value his hand before any bid has been made, and how to judge whether he should pass on it or open the bidding.

HIGH- AND LOW-CARD TRICKS

There are two standards by which a hand may be valued: it may be strong in honour cards, or it may contain long and powerful suits and be strong distributionally. Consider the following hands:

A.	B.	C.
♠—K J 10 7 6 4 2	♠—A Q 8 3	♠—A K 8 6 4 2
♡—8 5	♡—A 4	♡—10 5
◇—9 6 4	◇—A 7 5 2	◇—A Q 7
♣—2	♣—6 5 4	♣—8 4

Hand A has only distributional strength. If Spades are trumps, it will be worth several tricks, but otherwise it will be worth little or nothing. Hand B is not strong in distribution but it has three Aces and a Queen. Hand C has strength of both kinds, a strong suit of Spades and some honour cards.

Bidding at contract is a partnership enterprise, and it is universally accepted that when a player opens the bidding with a call of One he should have a fair amount of high card strength. Generally speaking, a player should not open unless he has $2\frac{1}{2}$ or 3 certain tricks in high cards. That is the foundation upon which constructive bidding between partners is based. There follows a table of honour tricks which will show what you can count for various high-card combinations:

$$
\begin{aligned}
\text{A K} &= 2 \quad \text{Honour Tricks} \\
\text{K Q J} &= 1\tfrac{1}{2} \quad ,, \qquad ,, \\
\text{A Q} &= 1\tfrac{1}{2} \quad ,, \qquad ,, \\
\text{A} &= 1 \quad ,, \qquad ,, \\
\text{K Q} &= 1 \quad ,, \qquad ,, \\
\text{K x} &= \tfrac{1}{2} \quad ,, \qquad ,, \\
\text{Q J} &= \tfrac{1}{2} \quad ,, \qquad ,, \\
\end{aligned}
$$

You will observe that these figures are all based on commonsense expectation. Clearly an Ace is one high-card trick, and so is a K Q, because when the Ace is forced out the other Honour must win. K x is calculated as half, because sometimes the King will win a full trick and sometimes not.

Not all combinations of honours are included in the table above, but the value of others can easily be deduced. For example, if you have a guarded Queen it represents a plus value and two guarded Queens could be counted as a $\frac{1}{2}$ H.T. It is important to realise that not more than two H.T. can be counted for any one suit. If you have a suit consisting of A K Q J 6 4, clearly that suit should win six tricks in the play if the suit is trumps. On the other hand, if another suit is trumps, only the Ace and King are likely to be made. Therefore only 2 H.T. can be credited to this holding, because honour tricks are tricks likely to be made whatever the declaration may be.

To open the bidding the player should normally have not less than $2\frac{1}{2}$ H.T. and a fair five-card suit. If he has only four-card suits, he should have 3 to $3\frac{1}{2}$ H.T. Some borderline hands follow :

	A.		B.		C.
♠—K 5		♠—A 9		♠—K Q 5 2	
♡—A Q 10 9 6		♡—Q J 9 7 6		♡—A 8	
◇—8 5 4 3		◇—K Q 8		◇—K 6 4 3	
♣—6 2		♣—Q 7 4		♣—7 5 2	

Hand A contains a fair five-card suit but only 2 H.T. and should therefore be passed. Hand B has $2\frac{1}{2}$ H.T. and a five-card suit; bid One Heart. Hand C—$2\frac{1}{2}$ H.T. but only a four-card suit; not worth an opening bid.

	D.		E.		F.
♠—J 7		♠—8		♠—K 6 4 3	
♡—K Q 10 8 6		♡—A K 10 5		♡—A Q 8	
◇—A K J 5 3		◇—K Q 7 5 3		◇—K 7 2	
♣—2		♣—A 4 2		♣—K 10 8	

Hand D:—Bid One Heart, preferring the higher valued of the two suits of equal length. The fact that the Diamonds are slightly stronger is beside the point. Hand E:—Bid One Diamond because the Diamonds are longer than the Hearts. Hand F:—Bid One No-Trump as there is strength in every suit and the Spade suit is not good enough for an opening bid. A minor suit can be bid on a holding as weak as K x x x, but a four-card major suit should contain two honours not lower than the Jack, a minimum being Q J x x.

G.	H.	I.
♠—A Q 7 2	♠—Q 6 2	♠—Q 7 3
♡—8 4	♡—8	♡—K Q 8
◇—K J 7 5	◇—K Q 5	◇—A J 4
♣—K 9 2	♣—A J 9 6 4 2	♣—Q 7 6 2

Hand G should be opened One Diamond rather than One Spade. On minimum hands like this one with two four-card suits, the lower suit is the safer bid if the suits are not adjacent. This is an exception to the general rule that between suits of equal length the higher valued should be called first. Hand H can be opened One Club, for although it is just short of 2½ H.T. it contains a good six-card suit. Hand I :—If not vulnerable, One No-Trump can be bid, but if vulnerable, One Club is safer, for a vulnerable No-Trump should be somewhat stronger than this.

A good exercise for the reader at this point would be to deal four hands and estimate how many honour tricks each hand contains, whether it is good enough for an opening bid, and what the opening bid should be. Remember that the ordinary requirements are 2½ H.T. with a fair five-card suit, or 3 to 3½ H.T. when only a four-card suit is held. One No-Trump can be bid on hands of a balanced pattern containing 3 to 3½ H.T. non-vulnerable and 4 to 4½ H.T. vulnerable. A

No-Trump opening should be avoided on a hand which contains any suit as weak as two small cards.

THE LIMITS OF OPENING ONE BIDS

Of the hands given in this chapter none has been very strong. It is quite possible, however, for a hand to have as many as six honour tricks and still be a One bid. Only exceptional hands are opened with a call of more than One, and these are discussed in Chapter VII. It is possible to make a bid of One on a very strong hand without fear of missing game, because your partner will keep the bidding open on very slight values. An account of his responses to your opening One bid is the subject of the next chapter.

❦

CHAPTER V

THE FIRST RESPONSE TO BIDS OF ONE

THE partner of the opening bidder is referred to as the " responder." Assuming for the moment that the opening bid of One in a suit is not overcalled by the opponent, the responder's hand will fall into one of the following categories :

A. Denial bid.	Pass.
B. Weak bids of limited strength.	One No-Trump A single raise of the suit bid.
C. Bids of variable strength.	A bid of One in a higher ranking suit. A bid of Two in a lower ranking suit.
D. Strong bids inviting game.	Two No-Trumps. A double raise of the suit bid.

E. Game-going bids.	{	Three No-Trumps. A raise to game in the suit bid.
F. Game-forcing bids of unlimited strength	{	A jump bid in a new suit, such as Two Spades over One Heart, or Three Clubs over One Diamond.
G. Pre-emptive bids in a different suit.	{	Occasionally a high shut-out bid is in order, such as Four Hearts over One Diamond.

It will happen in many cases that the responding hand offers a suitable bid in more than one of the above categories. Sometimes a bid of a certain type is clearly indicated, sometimes there are several alternatives. The principles which should govern the selection of a bid will appear as the various responses are discussed.

THE PASS

As was remarked at the end of the last chapter, an opening bid of One may be made on a very powerful hand. For this reason an effort should always be made to keep the bidding open on hands of moderate strength, as will be seen in the next section. It is, however, correct to pass when the hand contains not more than one bare honour trick, has no fair suit which can be called to the level of One, and has no values in support of partner's suit. The following hands should be passed in response to an opening bid of One Spade :

$\spadesuit$—10 7 5 $\spadesuit$—6 $\spadesuit$—8 5 4
$\heartsuit$—K 8 6 $\heartsuit$—J 7 4 3 $\heartsuit$—A J 6
$\diamondsuit$—8 6 5 3 2 $\diamondsuit$—K 8 6 4 $\diamondsuit$—10 6 4 2
$\clubsuit$—Q 9 $\clubsuit$—9 6 5 2 $\clubsuit$—7 5 3

These hands represent *maximum* passes; a slight addition in strength would in each case make them proper responses.

One No-Trump

One No-Trump is the standard response on hands which contain from one to two honour tricks, no suit worth bidding, and not sufficient distributional values for a raise of the suit bid. The following are typical One No-Trump responses to an opening bid of One Heart:

♠—Q 7 6   ♠—J 6 4   ♠—K 8 2
♡—J 8 5   ♡—10 5   ♡—9 5 3 2
♢—10 9 4 3   ♢—K 8 7 6 3 ♢—Q 7 6
♣—A 8 2   ♣—K 9 4   ♣—K 8 4

It will be noticed that one of these hands contains a five-card Diamond suit. However, the hand is not strong enough for the comparatively encouraging response of Two Diamonds, and One No-Trump is the right response. The third hand has four cards of partner's suit and so qualifies for a raise of partner's One Heart bid to Two Hearts, but the pattern of the hand is so balanced that One No-Trump is a more accurate bid.

A Single Raise

The first requirement for a raise of partner's suit is adequate trump support. For a single raise to Two in the suit, four small cards are enough or three cards headed by two of the three top honours. *In no circumstances whatsoever should an immediate raise be given on three small cards or on two cards, even though they be Ace and King.*

In addition to honour tricks and length in trumps, the responding hand may have another element of strength in the form of ruffing values. To ruff is the same as to trump, and to possess ruffing values is to have a short side suit in which it is reasonable to suppose that partner can obtain ruffs. You will understand the meaning of this if you imagine these two hands in partnership :

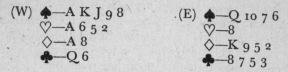

(W) ♠—A K J 9 8   (E) ♠—Q 10 7 6
     ♡—A 6 5 2   ♡—8
     ◇—A 8   ◇—K 9 5 2
     ♣—Q 6   ♣—8 7 5 3

If these hands play together at a contract of Four Spades, they should have no difficulty in making five.   There are two losers in Clubs but none in any other suit. Declarer would not draw trumps, but would play the Ace of Hearts and then a small Heart which dummy would ruff.   Declarer would regain the lead with the Ace of Diamonds and ruff a second Heart; he would then get back to his own hand once more by ruffing the third round of either Diamonds or Clubs, and would lead the fourth Heart and trump again in dummy.

You will notice that in the play of this hand the dummy has been worth a lot of tricks because of the ruffing values which it possessed through the combination of a singleton Heart and four trumps.   In valuing a hand for the purpose of raising partner's suit, therefore, equal importance must be attached to ruffing values as to honour tricks.   So long as four trumps are held a raise can be given with only half an honour trick if the hand contains a singleton.

♠—10 8 6 4   ♠—K 7 6 4   ♠—9 7 6 4 3
♡—K 7 5 2   ♡—K 8 4 2   ♡—10 9 2
◇—3   ◇—10 3   ◇— —
♣—J 9 5 2   ♣—8 7 2   ♣—8 6 4 3 2

These three hands all represent minimum raises of One Spade to Two Spades.   The third hand contains no honour tricks whatever; nevertheless it is a sound raise owing to its distributional values.   The five trumps in conjunction with the void are sure to win many tricks in the play.

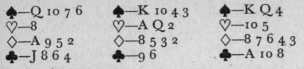

♠—Q 10 7 6   ♠—K 10 4 3   ♠—K Q 4
♡—8   ♡—A Q 2   ♡—10 5
◇—A 9 5 2   ◇—8 5 3 2   ◇—8 7 6 4 3
♣—J 8 6 4   ♣—9 6   ♣—A 10 8

These are rather stronger hands. They represent maximum holdings for a raise of One Spade to Two Spades.

Enough examples have been given to show the type of hand suitable for a single raise in your partner's suit. Like the response of One No-Trump, the single raise is a bid of strictly limited strength and it conveys precise information—trump support, not more than two honour tricks, and generally a singleton or doubleton in a side suit.

Simple Overcalls in a New Suit

The most informative response to an opening bid is always a bid in a new suit. If you have a minimum of one honour trick and have a fair suit which you can bid at the range of One, you need consider no other call. The following hands represent some minimum responses to an opening bid of One Diamond:

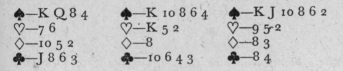

♠—K Q 8 4   ♠—K 10 8 6 4   ♠—K J 10 8 6 2
♡—7 6   ♡—K 5 2   ♡—9 5 2
◇—10 5 2   ◇—8   ◇—8 3
♣—J 8 6 3   ♣—10 6 4 3   ♣—8 4

On each of these hands One Spade should be bid. The third hand contains less than one honour trick, but the length of the Spade suit justifies a response.

If two suits are held, the same principles apply as determine the choice of an opening call. As a rule, bid the longer suit first, and where the suits are of equal length bid the higher ranking.

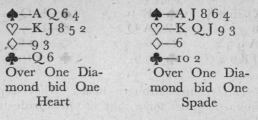

♠—A Q 6 4   ♠—A J 8 6 4
♡—K J 8 5 2   ♡—K Q J 9 3
◊—9 3   ◊—6
♣—Q 6   ♣—10 2

Over One Dia-   Over One Diamond bid One   mond bid One
Heart   Spade

For a bid of Two in a lower ranking suit slightly greater strength is required. The ordinary requirements are a five-card suit with $1\frac{1}{2}$ honour tricks or a six-card suit with one honour trick. The following are minimum hands for a response of this kind:

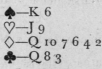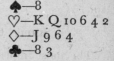

♠—K 8   ♠—K 6   ♠—8
♡—Q J 10 6 2   ♡—J 9   ♡—K Q 10 6 4 2
◊—10 4   ◊—Q 10 7 6 4 2 ◊—J 9 6 4
♣—K 8 6 3   ♣—Q 8 3   ♣—8 3

Over One Spade   Over One Heart   Over One Spade
bid Two Hearts   bid Two Diamonds bid Two Hearts

On a hand of this type :

♠—K 8
♡—Q J 7 6 3
◊—8 4 2
♣—Q 8 6

One Heart would be the right response to One Diamond; but if the opening bid is One Spade, One No-Trump is a sounder response than Two Hearts.

Choice between Overcall and Raise

It often happens that a hand qualifies both for a suit response and for a raise. If partner's suit is a major suit—Spades or Hearts—a raise should generally be

preferred, especially with four trumps.   But in responding to a minor suit it is better to show a new suit, since
game is difficult to make in the minor suit and other
possibilities should be explored.   With ♠—K J 6 4,
♡—J 7 5 3, ◇—8 2, ♣—A 8 6, One Heart should be
raised to Two Hearts, but over One Club the response
of One Spade is much more constructive than a raise to
Two Clubs.

A Response of Two No-Trumps

A response of Two No-Trumps shows an evenly
distributed hand with about $2\frac{1}{2}$ to 3 honour tricks.

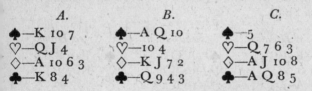

A.	*B.*	*C.*
♠—K 10 7	♠—A Q 10	♠—5
♡—Q J 4	♡—10 4	♡—Q 7 6 3
◇—A 10 6 3	◇—K J 7 2	◇—A J 10 8
♣—K 8 4	♣—Q 9 4 3	♣—A Q 8 5

Hand A represents a typical Two No-Trump response
to any One bid including One Diamond, for although
the Diamonds could be supported, Two No-Trumps is
both more informative and more constructive than
Three Diamonds.

On Hand B Two No-Trumps could be bid over One
Heart, but not over any other bid because of the weakness in Hearts.   Over One Spade, Two Diamonds
should be bid, and the Spades supported on the next
round.

On Hand C Two No-Trumps should be avoided even
if the opening is One Spade.   To have a singleton of
partner's suit is a distinct handicap in No-Trump play,
and an attempt should be made to find a better fit.   The
response to One Spade should be Two Diamonds.   If
the opener then bids Two Spades, Two No-Trumps has
to be tried on the second round, but if partner can bid

Hearts or Clubs an excellent fit is established, and the second suit can be raised to game.

A Double Raise

For a double raise of partner's bid from One to Three, trump support should be not less than four cards or three cards with two high honours. If in addition to good trump support a hand contains $2\frac{1}{2}$ honour tricks and a doubleton, or two honour tricks and a singleton, it is about right for a double raise. If the distributional support is exceptionally strong, the high card requirements are correspondingly reduced. The following hands all warrant a raise to Three of an opening bid of One Spade:

1st Hand.	. 2nd Hand.	3rd Hand.
♠—K J 6 4	♠—A Q 8	♠—J 10 8 6 2
♡—8	♡—10	♡—K 5 3
◇—A 9 5 2	◇—10 6 5 3 2	◇— —
♣—Q J 6 4	♣—A Q 10 4	♣—Q 9 8 6 2

A double raise of a minor suit should not be given immediately if there are any possibilities of exploring a major suit or No-Trump contract. These two hands are proper raises of One Diamond to Three Diamonds because no more constructive call is available:

1st Hand.	2nd Hand.
♠—8	♠—10 8 6 4
♡—J 9 3	♡—Q
◇—A 10 7 6 4	◇—K Q 6 4
♣—K J 5 2	♣—A 9 5 3

A Response of Three No-Trumps

A Three No-Trump response shows a strong balanced hand with 3 to 4 honour tricks. Some strength should be held in all the unb'd suits, and the holding in partner's suit should be not less than three small cards or Q x. The following hands warrant a bid of Three No-Trumps over any One bid:

♠—K Q 6	♠—A Q
♡—A 10 8	♡—K J 4
◇—K 9 5 2	◇—K 8 6 2
♣—Q J 3	♣—K 10 4 3

A RAISE TO GAME

A raise to game in a major suit is given on hands which are somewhat stronger than is required for a double raise. The following are sound raises of One Heart to Four Hearts:

1st Hand.	*2nd Hand.*	*3rd Hand.*
♠—8	♠—A 8 6 4	♠—A
♡—K 10 5 2	♡—Q J 9 5 2	♡—K 10 6 4
◇—A Q 8 5	◇—8	◇—K 9 7 6 3
♣—K 10 6 4	♣—A J 3	♣—K 5 2

A raise to game in a minor suit is given on hands which are exceptionally strong in support of partner's suit and extend no hope of game at No-Trumps. A raise of One Diamond to Five Diamonds would be in order on either of these hands:

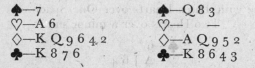

♠—7	♠—Q 8 3
♡—A 6	♡— —
◇—K Q 9 6 4 2	◇—A Q 9 5 2
♣—K 8 7 6	♣—K 8 6 4 3

GAME-FORCING BIDS IN A NEW SUIT

Sometimes the responder has a hand so strong that when his partner opens the bidding he can be confident that the combined hands contain sufficient strength for game at some contract.   Provided that his hand meets certain honour-trick requirements he can then make what is called a forcing bid, the effect of which is that the hands are committed to at least a game contract, and neither partner can drop the bidding until game has been reached.   The advantage of having forcing bids is that great strength can be shown at once and the subsequent bidding can be developed gradually without fear of its dying short of game, except possibly for a promising double of the opponents if they are rash enough to intervene.   Over an opening bid by partner a forcing bid is a bid of one more than is necessary in some suit other than the one which has been called. Thus over One Diamond, Two Hearts is forcing to game, or over One Spade, Three Hearts.

To qualify for a forcing response a hand should contain at least 3 honour tricks with strong distribution, or upwards of $3\frac{1}{2}$ honour tricks.   A simple take-out into a new suit always elicits at least one more bid from the opener, so there is no need to force every time it appears that the combined hands are worth a game contract. The following hands illustrate minimum forces:

♠—K 6
♡—A Q J 8 4 2
♢—A Q 3
♣—8 4

Force with Three Hearts over One Spade or with Two Hearts over a minor suit.

♠—9
♡—A J 6 4
♢—A K 6 4 2
♣—J 5 3

Force with Three Diamonds over One Heart but over One Spade bid only Two Diamonds, as you do not

want to crowd the bidding until you have found the best
contract.

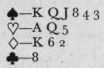

♠—K Q J 8 4 3
♡—A Q 5
◇—K 6 2
♣—8

Force with Two Spades over any One bid.

♠—K Q 5 2
♡—K 8 6 3
◇—A Q
♣—A 6 2

Over One Spade the right bid is a force of Three
Clubs. Of course you have no intention of playing
in Clubs, but you are far too strong for a bid of Four
Spades which may well be passed. In these circumstances it is quite safe to force in a lower-valued suit,
as you can always return to Spades if partner supports
the Club. It is better to bid Three Clubs and see how
the bidding develops, than to bid Five or Six Spades
right away.

Pre-emptive Bids in a Different Suit

Occasionally it is in order to jump straight to game in
another suit. This is done to show great strength in the
suit, and not much in the way of honour tricks. Thus,
if partner bids One Diamond, and second hand passes,
you should bid Four Hearts on ♠—8, ♡—K Q 10
9 7 6 4 2, ◇—Q 3, ♣—6 2. Note that although
this bid of Four Hearts is at a higher range than a
forcing bid of Two Hearts, it shows much less strength
in high cards. One object of the bid is to make it
difficult for the opponents to get together in Spades
which they may hold strongly. That explains the word
" pre-emptive " which is used to describe shut-out bids

of this kind. They are designed to *buy* the contract *before* the opponents have a chance to get together.

THE EFFECT OF AN INTERVENING CALL

One effect of an intervening call by second hand is that the responder is relieved of the responsibility of keeping the bidding open for his partner on minimum values. Holding ♠—10 8, ♡—K J 6 4, ◇—Q 9 5 2, ♣—J 8 3, if partner were to open One Club, you would respond One Heart if there were no intervening call, but if second hand were to bid One Spade, you should pass, as partner is automatically given another chance to speak, and any free bid by you would show fair strength. In the same way, if partner opened One Spade, you should normally respond One No-Trump on this hand, but if second hand were to make any overcall you should pass.

To bid One No-Trump over an intervening suit call it is important that you should have a holding in the suit strong enough to prevent the opponents running off several tricks at a No-Trump contract. If you hold ♠—K 10 6, ♡—10 5 2, ◇—Q J 3, ♣—A 6 4 2, and partner opens One Diamond and second hand bids One Spade, you can say One No-Trump, as you have a guard in Spades. But if second hand bids One Heart, you cannot bid One No-Trump as you have no strength in Hearts; you must bid Two Diamonds or possibly Two Clubs.

RESPONDING TO ONE NO-TRUMP

Partner's opening bid of One No-Trump gives a fairly exact account of his holding, a balanced hand with about 3 to 3½ honour tricks not vulnerable, and about 3½ to 4 vulnerable. If the responder's hand is also of an even distribution, he will raise the No-Trump bid. The

following hands are of the approximate strength needed
for raises to Two or Three No-Trumps :

Hand A.	Hand B.
♠—K 10 6 2	♠—A 8 4
♡—8 5	♡—K 10 5 3
◇—A 7 6 4	◇—10 8
♣—Q J 3	♣—J 9 7 6

Hand A warrants a raise to Two No-Trumps non-
vulnerable and to Three No-Trumps vulnerable because
partner is known to be somewhat stronger.

Hand B should be passed non-vulnerable, but a
vulnerable No-Trump can be raised to two. It is
impossible to define in terms of honour tricks the strength
necessary for raises in No-Trumps, because intermediate
cards like Jacks, Tens, and Nines are worth a good deal
more at No-Trump play than at suit play. For example,
this hand, ♠—A J 9, ♡—Q 10 8 4, ◇—J 10 7, ♣—K 9 4,
contains only two honour tricks even if you count in all
the Queens and Jacks, but it is a much stronger hand in
support of a No-Trump opening than a hand like this :
♠—A K 6, ♡—8 5 4 2, ◇—6 5 4, ♣—K 8 3. On the
former hand a raise to Three No-Trumps should be given
even if non-vulnerable, but the latter hand is hardly
worth a raise to Two No-Trumps non-vulnerable unless
partner is known to make rather strong No-Trump calls.

If the responder's hand is unbalanced, he should take
out into a suit call. If his hand is weak and does not
offer a possibility of game, he should make a simple
take-out into Two of his suit. If he thinks a game
contract is on, he should make a jump bid.

Hand A.	Hand B.	Hand C.
♠—J 9 7 6 4 2	♠—K 10 7 6 2	♠—Q J 3
♡—3	♡—Q 5	♡—K 10 7 6 2
◇—Q 6 2	◇—J 8 3	◇—A 10 8 3
♣—8 5 3	♣—A Q 3	♣—Q

On Hand A the responder should take out into Two Spades. A sensible partner will not regard this as a strength-showing bid. To pass One No-Trump is likely to produce a very bad result, for the hand may well prove useless unless Spades are trumps.

Although Hand B contains a five-card major suit, the best bid is a raise to Three No-Trumps. This is because the hand will play equally well in No-Trumps or Spades, and there is no point in attempting to steer the contract into Four Spades rather than into Three No-Trumps.

On Hand C a jump to Three Hearts should be given. This bid is forcing on the opener who will bid either Three No-Trumps or Four Hearts. Note, however, that the forcing response to the No-Trump opening does not convey the same implications of high-card strength as the forcing response to an opening suit bid.

When the responder's hand contains a long suit in which he is prepared to play for game, he can make a direct game bid.

♠—K J 7 6 4 3
♡—3
♢—A J 5 2
♣—10 8

This hand offers a play for game in conjunction with a No-Trump opening, and a direct response of Four Spades is in order.

CHAPTER VI

THE FIRST REBID BY THE OPENING BIDDER

IF partner has responded to an opening bid of One, the opening bidder has to consider his hand from two angles. He must ask himself, (1) does my hand contain any appreciable values beyond those indicated by my opening bid ? and (2) does my hand contain any appreciable extra values when viewed as support for my partner's declaration ?

The answers to these questions are not always the same. Suppose you open One Spade on:

♠—A K 9 5 2
♡—K 10 5 3
♢—8 4
♣—J 5

and partner responds with a bid of Two Hearts. Now, considered as an opening One Spade bid your hand is a complete minimum, but when reviewed as a supporting hand for partner's Heart bid it reveals appreciable extra values and is obviously worth a raise. In the discussion which follows, the opener's rebid is analysed in face of each of the responses classified in the last chapter. It will be found throughout that the rebid is determined by the answers to the two questions stated above.

WHEN PARTNER RESPONDS WITH ONE NO-TRUMP

Ask yourself first of all, how much strength has partner shown ? The answer is that he has shown a balanced hand of moderate strength with from one to two honour tricks. To encourage a game bid at No-Trumps, therefore, you must have a powerful hand of $3\frac{1}{2}$ to $4\frac{1}{2}$ honour tricks.

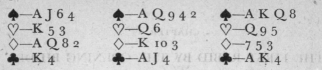

♠—A J 6 4   ♠—A Q 9 4 2   ♠—A K Q 8
♡—K 5 3   ♡—Q 6   ♡—Q 9 5
◇—A Q 8 2   ◇—K 10 3   ◇—7 5 3
♣—K 4   ♣—A J 4   ♣—A K 4

On each of these hands you open One Spade and partner responds with One No-Trump. In each case you can raise to Two No-Trumps, which invites partner to bid Three unless his first response was a complete minimum. Had any of these hands been weaker by as much as a Queen, you would have had to pass the response of One No-Trump. One of the commonest mistakes made by beginners is to over-value their hands in face of a One No-Trump response. To encourage a game bid in face of a One No-Trump response the opener should have a full honour trick over and above what was needed for an opening bid.

♠—K 8   ♠—Q 10 3
♡—A 10 5   ♡—A Q 4
◇—A K 6 4 2   ◇—A K 6 4
♣—K J 10   ♣—K J 5

These two hands are a little stronger. Having opened One Diamond and had a One No-Trump response, you can bid Three No-Trumps.

On unbalanced hands containing a singleton it is generally advisable to take out One No-Trump into your own long suit, or if you have a two-suit hand, into your second suit.

♠—Q J 8 7 5 2   ♠—8
♡—9   ♡—Q J 6 4 2
◇—A 8 4   ◇—A Q 7 6 4
♣—A J 3   ♣—A J

These hands are not suitable for play in No-Trumps, and on the first you should rebid Two Spades and on the second Two Diamonds.

♠—K 8   ♠—A Q 6 4
♡—A K 7 6 3   ♡—A Q 5 2
♢—Q 5 2   ♢—10 8
♣—J 10 3   ♣—Q 6 3

On these two hands you should pass a One No-Trump response, for although one contains a five-card suit and the other has a second biddable suit, both hands are suitable for play in No-Trumps, and it would be a mistake to disturb the contract.

Stronger hands may call for a jump rebid of your first suit or a jump bid in another suit. This jump bid in a new suit is unconditionally forcing to game.

Hand A.   *Hand B.*
♠—A Q J 7 6 3   ♠—A Q J 6 4
♡—8 5   ♡—A K 7 5 2
♢—A Q 2   ♢—K 3
♣—K 3   ♣—10

Hand A calls for a jump rebid of Three Spades, strongly inviting partner to bid either Four Spades or Three No-Trumps. Hand B justifies a forcing bid of Three Hearts, compelling partner to take further action either by supporting one of your suits, or by bidding Three No-Trumps.

When Partner Raises Your Bid

If partner raises your suit bid, your course of action is generally fairly clear. If he gives you a simple raise only, you pass unless your hand contains appreciable extra values.

♠—A Q 10 5   ♠—A J 8 3
♡—8 3   ♡—A Q 6 2
◊—A K 6   ◊—K 8
♣—Q 9 4 2   ♣—10 6 4

On both these hands you should pass if your opening bid of One Spade is raised to Two Spades.

If your hand appears to offer chances of game, but you do not care to bid it yourself without learning something more about your partner's hand, you can bid Two No-Trumps, Three of the suit, or Three of another suit.

A.   B.   C.

♠—A Q 10 7 4 2   ♠—A J 9 7   ♠—A Q 7 6 4
♡—A Q 10   ♡—K 4   ♡—8
◊—J 5   ◊—K J 9 2   ◊—K J 10 8
♣—6 2   ♣—K Q 3   ♣—A 10 2

Suppose that on each of these hands you have opened One Spade and partner has raised to Two Spades. In each case you feel you are worth another try, and yet you should not bid game yourself in case partner's raise was a minimum. On Hand A you can do nothing more helpful than bid Three Spades. On Hand B you can say Two No-Trumps, and if partner bids Three No-Trumps you will pass, and you will also pass if he denies any further values by bidding Three Spades. If his raise was a good one, he should bid Four Spades. On Hand C you should bid Three Diamonds; partner should realise that you are exploring game possibilities and should never leave you in this call after he has raised One Spade. If he is weak, he will bid Three Spades which you will pass, but if he has a fair raise and a fit in Diamonds, he will bid Four Spades.

WHEN PARTNER RESPONDS WITH TWO NO-TRUMPS

This response you should pass only if your opening was a dead minimum. Any fair opening hand in conjunction with a Two No-Trump response should offer a play for game.

If your hand is weak, but your suit is rebiddable, you should bid Three of it, warning partner that you do not fancy the chances of a game bid.

```
♠—K Q 10 7 4 2
♡—A J
◇—8 6 4
♣—9 3
```

Over Two No-Trumps you rebid Three Spades, which partner should pass unless he has reserve values in support of Spades. It follows that if your hand is somewhat stronger, say by an extra King in one of the minor suits, you should rebid Four Spades.

WHEN PARTNER MAKES A SIMPLE OVERCALL

When partner makes a simple overcall in a new suit, a wide range of rebids is offered. The opening bidder must study his hand carefully to see what reserves of strength he has. If his opening bid was not far from a minimum, he will rebid in such a way as to show this by bidding One No-Trump, making a simple rebid of his own suit, giving a single raise of his partner's suit, or bidding a second suit himself. The most helpful bid, if the values for it exist, is a raise of partner's suit.

```
♠—8
♡—K J 5
◇—A 10 7 6 2
♣—A J 5 3
```

You open One Diamond on this hand and partner responds One Spade. You might say One No-Trump, but as you have a singleton Spade it is preferable to bid Two Clubs. If over your One Diamond partner bids One Heart, you should raise to Two Hearts rather than bid Two Clubs. If partner's response is Two Clubs, you will raise to Three Clubs.

With stronger hands you can rebid Two or Three No-Trumps, give a jump raise of partner's suit, or a jump rebid of your own suit.

♠—Q 8
♡—K Q 4
◊—A J 7 3 2
♣—A J 8

You bid One Diamond and partner responds One Spade. You have a full trick above a minimum opening and can rebid Two No-Trumps.

If partner's response is made at the level of Two, you should still have more than a minimum for a rebid of Two No-Trumps.

	A.		*B.*
♠—A J 6 2		♠—A J 6 2	
♡—K 5		♡—7 5	
◊—K 8 3		◊—K 8 3	
♣—K Q 10 4		♣—K Q 10 4	

On Hand A you open One Spade and partner responds Two Hearts. Having about a King above a minimum opening, you can make the constructive rebid of Two No-Trumps.

If on Hand B you were to open One Spade, and partner were to respond Two Hearts, you would not be entitled to rebid Two No-Trumps, for you have a dead minimum opening. Still less would it be in order to carry the bidding to the range of Three by calling Three Clubs. It appears, therefore, that you have no sound rebid, and yet you are not allowed to pass this suit response by partner. The answer is that you made the wrong opening bid. As was remarked in Chapter IV, on weak hands containing only four-card suits the lower-valued should be bid first unless the suits are adjacent. On the present hand the only sound opening is One Club, and then if partner bids One Heart you can say One Spade without raising the level of the bidding.

Hand A.

♠—K J 10 4
♡—A 5 2
◇—A Q 7 6 3
♣—8

Hand B.

♠—9 4
♡—A Q J 7 6 2
◇—A Q 10
♣—K 8

On Hand A you open One Diamond and partner responds One Spade. Your hand has considerable reserves of strength when reviewed in support of partner's call and you should raise to Three Spades.

On Hand B your rebid over a response of One Spade would be a jump to Three Hearts. These jump raises and jump rebids are not forcing on partner, but they strongly encourage him to bid to game.

When your hand is so strong that once partner responds you are determined to reach game, you must either bid the game direct or make a forcing rebid by means of a jump bid in a new suit.

♠—A Q 10 5 2
♡—A K 8 5 3
◇—A 4
♣—2

You open One Spade and partner responds One No-Trump or Two Diamonds. In either case you should make a forcing rebid of Three Hearts.

CHAPTER VII

OPENING BIDS OF MORE THAN ONE

OPENING bids of One are best for the great majority of hands. The lower the bidding starts the more time there is for the exchange of information which should lead to the best contract. A few hands, however, are so strong that the risk cannot be taken that partner will pass a bid of One. These are opened with a Forcing Two bid. Other hands which contain long and strong suits and not much else are opened with pre-emptive bids of Three and Four, and a few hands with all-round strength are opened with Two or Three No-Trumps.

THE FORCING TWO BID

An opening bid of Two in a suit is forcing to game. That is, of course, a convention. There is nothing in the laws of the game to say that a bid of Two should be forcing, but it is one of the conventions of the approach forcing system on which this book is based. This general system of bidding is in fact often known as the Forcing Two.

To open with a forcing bid the player should as a rule hold five honour tricks and also hold sufficient playing tricks in his own hand to ensure that a game bid (which must be reached) will not be heavily defeated.

Some examples follow which show how carefully these bids must be handled.

	A.		*B.*		*C.*
♠—	K Q 4	♠—	7 2	♠—	K Q 7 6 4
♡—	7 3	♡—	A K 6 5	♡—	A K
◇—	A K J 5	◇—	A K 3	◇—	A K 6
♣—	A K 10 9	♣—	A K 8 3	♣—	7 4 3

Hand A has five honour tricks and some useful plus values, but if you open with a bid of Two Diamonds, how far will you get if partner turns up with nothing of value? If you are to make a game, partner must have at least a good enough hand to respond to One Diamond, so you need not think twice about this hand. Hand B has no fewer than six quick tricks—an irresistible lure to most players—but if partner passes a bid of One Heart, six tricks may be all that you will make. Hand C has five quick tricks and a fair five-card suit, but if partner cannot even say One No-Trump to a bid of One Spade, you know that his hand will not go far to cover your six losers—three clubs, one diamond, and two spades. So here again it would be wrong to make a forcing bid.

The following hands are sound Two bids:

	A.	*B.*	*C.*
♠	—A K J 5 2	—A K J 5	—6
♡	—A K 10 7 3	—K 8	—A Q J 10 7 4
♢	—8	—A K 6 2	—A K J 9 3
♣	—A 4	—A K 4	—A

Hand A only just qualifies for a forcing bid. If the Ace of Clubs were the King, it would be worth One Spade only. Hand B is not strongly distributed, but it holds too many high cards for a bid of One to be safe. Hand C contains only $4\frac{1}{2}$ honour tricks, but it is so powerful that Two Hearts should be bid. It is not advisable to open with a forcing bid on a hand which contains less than four honour tricks, however strong it is. Occasionally one picks up a hand of this type:

♠—A K J 9 6 4
♡—5
♢—K Q J 9 8 4
♣— —

Of course this hand is so powerful that you certainly do not want to play in less than a game contract. Many players would open Two Spades, but this is both unsound and unnecessary. It is unsound because if partner has a good hand he is almost sure to put you into an unmakable slam, as he will not dream that you hold only one Ace. It is unnecessary because there are several high cards out and it is most unlikely you would be left to play in One Spade. Another reason why a good player would not bid more than One Spade is that owing to the exceptional distribution of this hand it offers great scope for a psychological coup; provided that the strength of the hand is not crudely revealed, it should be possible to deceive the opponents and be doubled by them in a safe contract.

RESPONDING TO OPENING TWO BIDS

Remember that the partner of the player who opens with a forcing bid must not let the bidding die short of game. The weakness response is always a bid of No-Trumps. Therefore, if you hold nothing whatever of value, your response to a Two Bid is Two No-Trumps. If partner then bids another suit, you may be able to give him a preference, and if he rebids his first suit you may be able to give him a distributional raise. If you cannot do any of these things, you must again bid No-Trumps. The No-Trump bid is known as the negative response, and it should always be given on a hand which contains less than one honour trick

♠—10 7 6 5 4 2
♡—8
◇—K 6 4
♣—7 5 3

If partner opens Two Hearts, you must say Two No-Trumps, not Two Spades. You will be able to show your

Spades on the next round. At least one honour trick should be held before a positive response is made.

A.	B.	C.
♠—Q 8 4	♠—K Q 8 5 3	♠—7 6
♡—A 7 4 2	♡—6 4	♡—6 4
◇—8 5	◇—J 7 5 3	◇—K J 7 6 3
♣—10 6 4 2	♣—8 5	♣—Q 6 5 2

In each case the opening bid is Two Hearts. On Hand A you can give a simple raise to Three Hearts. On Hand B you can say Two Spades. Many players expect more for a positive response, some demanding an Ace and a King, but the modern tendency is to shade the requirements for a positive response to the lowest limit. Hand C, however, does not quite warrant a response in Diamonds at the level of Three, and therefore the response is Two No-Trumps.

OPENING BIDS OF THREE AND FOUR

No universal agreement exists as to the type of hand for which it is most useful to reserve an opening bid of Three in a suit. Some players will open Three Hearts on a powerful hand such as :

♠—7
♡—A K J 10 7 6 4
◇—K Q 6
♣—K 5

A more modern school prefers to use very weak Three bids, and will bid Three Spades on:

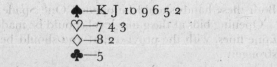

♠—K J 10 9 6 5 2
♡—7 4 3
◇—8 2
♣—5

The argument of the latter school is that if this bid of Three Spades is doubled and defeated the maximum of four tricks (for at least five trump tricks should be made), it follows that the opposition must have enough cards for a slam. Therefore the loss of 700 for four down doubled non-vulnerable represents a good save when set against what the opposition would have scored had they been given the chance to bid up undisturbed. For inexperienced players we recommend something between these two extremes. Opening bids of Three should be made on hands which will play well only in one suit and which contain six to seven playing tricks and at the most $2\frac{1}{2}$ honour tricks.

	A.		*B.*
♠—K Q J 10 6 4 2		♠—8	
♡—8		♡—7 3	
◇—8 5 3		◇—A K Q 7 6 4 2	
♣—K 4		♣—9 5 4	

A bid of Three could be made on either of these hands. But the following hands are not suitable for Three bids because they are too strong, and also because their strength is not concentrated in the one suit.

	A.		*B.*
♠—A J 10 9 7 6 4		♠—K Q J 8 4 3	
♡—K Q 3		♡—9	
◇—5		◇—A Q 5 2	
♣—K 2		♣—10 4	

Both these hands should be opened One Spade.

Opening bids at the game level should be made on the same lines, with the proviso that you should be a trick stronger.

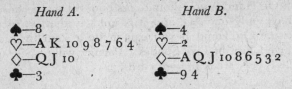

Hand A.
- ♠—8
- ♡—A K 10 9 8 7 6 4
- ◇—Q J 10
- ♣—3

Hand B.
- ♠—4
- ♡—2
- ◇—A Q J 10 8 6 5 3 2
- ♣—9 4

Hand A is a Four Heart bid. On Hand B you should pre-empt to the limit with a call of Five Diamonds.

RESPONDING TO BIDS OF THREE AND FOUR

If you understand partner's Three bids to be of the approximate strength of those given in the last section, you should raise to game on about 2½ to 3 honour tricks.

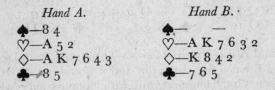

Hand A.
- ♠—8 4
- ♡—A 5 2
- ◇—A K 7 6 4 3
- ♣—8 5

Hand B.
- ♠—— —
- ♡—A K 7 6 3 2
- ◇—K 8 4 2
- ♣—7 6 5

On Hand A you can raise Three Spades to Four Spades. Of course the ordinary requirements for trump support are quite different when partner has shown a powerful suit. On Hand B you should pass Three Spades. Partner's Spades are no doubt stronger than your Hearts, and you should not fight his bid. It is very unlikely that he has any fit in Hearts.

To invite a slam over an opening Four bid you should hold 3½ to 4 honour tricks.

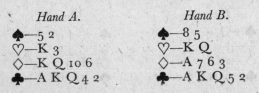

Hand A.
- ♠—5 2
- ♡—K 3
- ◇—K Q 10 6
- ♣—A K Q 4 2

Hand B.
- ♠—8 5
- ♡—K Q
- ◇—A 7 6 3
- ♣—A K Q 5 2

On Hand A you should pass Four Spades because you have only one Ace and it is unlikely that partner has two. On Hand B you can invite a slam by bidding Five Clubs or Five Spades. Partner will go Six, unless he is very weak in high cards.

OPENING BIDS OF TWO NO-TRUMPS

Two No-Trumps is a useful bid on hands of all-round strength and about $4\frac{1}{2}$ to 5 honour tricks which require only a smattering of high cards from partner for a fair chance of game.

A.	B.	C.
♠—A J 5	♠—A Q	♠—A 9 7 4
♡—A 10 6 4	♡—A J 3	♡—A K
◇—K Q 7	◇—K Q 10 8 4	◇—A J 7 3
♣—A Q 10	♣—K J 2	♣—K Q 6

Hand A is a typical Two No-Trump bid at any score. Hand B has a five-card suit, and it would not be wrong to open One Diamond, but with honours everywhere it is a sound tactical Two No-Trump bid. Hand C has enough honour tricks for a Two No-Trump bid and strength in every suit, but the make-up of the hand is better fitted for trump play as there are few honours in proportion to the strength of the hand; open One Diamond.

RESPONSES TO A TWO NO-TRUMP OPENING

Very little is required to raise Two No-Trumps to Three.

Hand A.	Hand B.
♠—Q 10 7	♠—7 4
♡—J 9 4 2	♡—5 3 2
◇—10 6	◇—K J 7 5 4
♣—Q 9 6 3	♣—10 6 2

These hands represent minimum raises. The raise on Hand B is possible by virtue of the five-card suit which is likely to prove very useful.

A simple take-out into Three of a suit will not be passed by the opening bidder as will a simple take-out of a One No-Trump bid.   A bid of Three of a suit can therefore be made on hands of widely differing character. The bid may be the beginning of a rescue into Four of a major suit, or it may be the beginning of a slam invitation.

Hand A.	*Hand B.*	*Hand C.*
♠—K 6	♠—10 7 6 5 3 2	♠—8
♡—Q 8 6 4 3	♡—9	♡—K J 9 7 2
◇—J 8	◇—K 6 3	◇—A 10 7 6 3
♣—10 7 6 3	♣—J 5 2	♣—K 5

Hand A—Bid Three Hearts, and if partner says Three No-Trumps, pass.

Hand B—Bid Three Spades and over Three No-Trumps, Four Spades.

Hand C—Bid Three Hearts and subsequently show the Diamonds: you intend to proceed to a slam on this hand, but there is no need to jump the bidding.

OPENING BIDS OF THREE NO-TRUMPS

Three No-Trumps should be bid on hands of great all-round strength and even distribution.   This is the type of hand best suited for the bid:

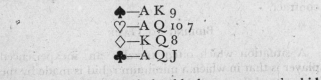

♠—A K 9
♡—A Q 10 7
◇—K Q 8
♣—A Q J

The responding hand should always rescue the bid of Three No-Trumps into Four of a major suit if the hand is weak but contains a long suit. There is not, or at least there should not be, any danger that the No-Trump bidder will regard this as a sign of strength and bid his hand again. With a hand of fair strength, offering slam possibilities, a jump bid should be made.

♠—8 7 6 4 3 2   ♠—6 2
♡—7   ♡—K 10 8 6 4
◇—J 7 6 3   ◇—10 5
♣—4 2   ♣—A J 4 2

Bid Four Spades   Bid Five Hearts
over Three   over Three
No-Trumps   No-Trumps

CHAPTER VIII

BIDDING TO GAME AND SLAM

THE last four chapters have given some account of the groundwork of constructive bidding. After the first three bids the variations are so numerous that it is impracticable to give a detailed description of the later rounds of the bidding. An attempt is made, however, in this chapter to give an inexperienced player an idea of how to judge whether game or slam is worth attempting or whether it is better to stay in a safe part-score contract.

BIDDING TO GAME

A situation which often puzzles an inexperienced player is that in which a minimum rebid is made by the opener and the responder has to judge whether or not to try for game.

♠—K 10 5
♡—A Q 8 2
◇—9 4
♣—K J 6 3

Partner opens One Diamond, and you make the natural response of One Heart. Now partner rebids One No-Trump. The responder should reason as follows: "Since my partner has rebid One No-Trump, he must have opened on a balanced hand and have fair all-round strength. I have practically the values for an opening bid myself, and as a No-Trump contract suits both players, I can bid a direct Three No-Trump." For it is a sound proposition that *whenever the two hands contain between them the values for two opening bids, a game should be possible, provided that a declaration can be found which suits both hands.*

Now let us suppose that the opener rebids Two Diamonds, and that the responder as before has bid One Heart over One Diamond on:

♠—K 6 5
♡—A Q 8 2
◇—9 4
♣—K J 6 3

Here it is sufficient to bid Two No-Trumps, inviting partner to bid Three No-Trumps if he has any strength in reserve. The reason why the responder should not bid Three No-Trumps this time is that partner may have a hand definitely unsuited to play at No-Trumps. If over Two No-Trumps partner signs off with Three Diamonds, responder should pass.

♠—8 4
♡—A 10 6 2
◇—K 5
♣—K 9 7 6 2

Partner opens One Spade and you respond Two Clubs. Now partner rebids Two No-Trumps. You may think that you have nothing in reserve, but in fact you should raise to Three No-Trumps. Partner's rebid of Two No-Trumps showed extra values to the extent of about one King. If you—in imagination—add this King to your own hand, you will find that you have the values for an opening bid, and you can therefore conclude that the two hands between them contain the values for two opening bids which, as we have said, puts them in the game zone.

♠—7 2
♡—A K 7 5 3
♢—5 4
♣—Q 8 6 2

Partner opens One Spade and you say Two Hearts. If partner rebids Two Spades, you should pass, for partner has shown no extra values apart from a rebiddable suit, and you have not the values for an opening bid yourself, nor have you anything much in the way of support for Spades. If you had had three spades and a singleton diamond, you would have bid Three Spades over Two Spades because of the ruffing values and support for the rebid suit.

♠—A J 9
♡—K 10 7 6 2
♢—10 5
♣—J 9 4

On this hand you respond One Heart to One Diamond. If partner rebids Two Diamonds, you should pass; if he rebids Two Hearts, you should also pass. If he rebids Two Clubs, however, you should give him a further chance by bidding Two No-Trumps. His Two Club rebid does not necessarily show extra values beyond the possession of a second biddable suit, but the Two Club bid is not a limited bid in the same way that Two Diamonds and Two Hearts are. It is quite possible that partner is only just short of the values needed for a forcing rebid. As you have fair strength to the unbid suit (Spades), you should certainly keep the bidding open with Two No-Trumps.

♠—Q 4
♡—7 5 2
♢—A K 8 5
♣—K J 6 2

Partner opens One Heart, and you say Two Diamonds. If partner rebids Two Hearts, you should bid Four Hearts, for you have just about the values for an opening bid, and you have adequate support for the rebid suit together with a likely ruffing value in Spades.

BIDDING TO SLAM

The first thing to know about slam bidding is the extent to which it is permissible to risk missing a game by bidding a problematical slam. Roughly speaking, a small slam may be bid on an even chance whether vulnerable or not. That is to say, the bonus you score for the successful slam is just about equal to the value of the game lost if the slam fails. A grand slam, however, should not be bid unless the odds are fully 2 to 1 in favour, for the extra bonus is not more than half the value of the game and small slam lost. In practice, therefore, a grand slam should be bid only when the player judges that it can hardly fail.

The art of slam bidding is highly complicated, and advanced players make use of all sorts of conventions to enable them to locate the controls necessary to a slam contract. Inexperienced players would do well to confine their attempts at slam bidding to hands whose combined strength clearly puts them in the slam zone.

A player may assume that a slam is likely if he can gauge that the two hands contain between them the values for an opening bid on one side, plus the values for a jump rebid on the other.

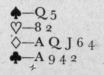

♠—Q 5
♡—8 2
◇—A Q J 6 4
♣—A 9 4 2

You respond Two Diamonds to One Spade, and partner rebids Three Spades. As you have the values for an opening bid yourself and partner has opened and made a jump rebid, you know that you can enter the slam zone. Your Queen of Spades is such an important card that you would not be out of order in going straight to Six Spades; at the very least you you should say Five Spades.

♠—A Q 7 6 4
♡—Q 5 2
◇—8 3
♣—A 6 4

Partner bids One Heart and you respond One Spade. Partner now follows with Three Diamonds. This is an even stronger rebid than Three Hearts or Three Spades, for it is forcing to game. Responder should for the moment bid simply Three Hearts; a forcing situation is in being and there is no need to crowd the bidding. It is quite likely that partner's force was based on strong support for Spades which he will show on the next round. Whether partner's next bid is in Hearts, Spades, or No-Trumps, you can raise to Six in whatever denomination he mentions.

♠—A 10 5 4 2
♡—Q 9 3
♢—8
♣—K 6 4 2

Partner opens with a forcing bid of Two Hearts. You respond Two Spades, and partner says Three Hearts. You should raise to Six, because in support of Hearts you have three useful honours, trump support and ruffing values. As partner must have nearly a game in his own hand to open with a forcing bid, it is obvious that with your wonderful support Six should be on.

When the responder has made a forcing take-out, the opener must always be on the look-out for a slam if he has something more than a minimum.

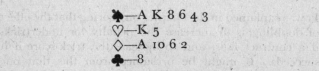

♠—A K 8 6 4 3
♡—K 5
♢—A 10 6 2
♣—8

You open with One Spade and partner forces with Three Hearts. You rebid Three Spades, and partner says Four Spades. You have quite a good-looking hand with a long trump suit, $3\frac{1}{2}$ honour tricks and second-round control of every suit. You can bid Six Spades with confidence.

BIDDING FROM A PART SCORE

A side which has a part score of 40 or over has only to make Two of a major or Three of a minor suit in order to score game. Possession of a part score makes very little difference to opening bids. It does not pay to make sub-minimum opening bids on the ground that there is not so far to go for game, nor is there any need to be over-cautious and pass minimum hands for fear of provoking opposition bidding.

Some players like to bid to the score, which means that if they make an opening Two bid which is enough to score game, such as Two Spades at 60 up, the Two bid is not to be regarded as forcing but simply as an attempt to buy the contract. It is more usual, however, not to vary the standards for Two bids. The responder should keep the bidding open for at least one round. In the same way, a forcing response such as Two Hearts over One Diamond at 40 up remains forcing for one round although game has been bid.

CHAPTER IX

PENALTY AND TAKE-OUT DOUBLES

IT was explained in the chapter on Scoring that the effect of doubling is to increase the penalty for undertricks if a contract fails, and to increase the trick score if it succeeds. It might be presumed from this that one would double only when one expected to defeat the opponents' contract. There is a convention, however, whereby in certain circumstances a double is made not for the purpose of increasing penalties, but in order to show a strong hand and to elicit a bid from partner. When a double is made for that reason it is called an " informatory " or " take-out " double. It is naturally of the utmost importance to distinguish between the two types of double, since to confuse them leads to all sorts of trouble. The following definition should make the distinction clear:

If partner has made a bid of any kind, at any time, and in any denomination, then any double by you is a penalty double, made with the expectation of defeating the contract.

If partner has not spoken, or has simply passed, a double of One or Two of a suit is for a take-out; a double of Two No-Trumps is always a penalty double.

A double of One No-Trump is equivocal. This double should only be made on strong hands, by themselves almost capable of defeating the contract, but if partner has a weak and unbalanced hand, he can take out the double.

A number of examples follow, illustrating the two types of double :

South.	*West.*	*North.*	*East.*
One Heart.	No.	Two Diamonds.	Double.

A take-out double, because partner had not made a bid.

One Heart.	One Spade.	Two Diamonds.	Double.

A penalty double, because partner has already shown his suit.

One Heart.	Double.	Two Diamonds.	Double.

West's double is for a take-out, East's for penalties.

One Heart.	Double.	Two Hearts.	No.
No.	Double.		

Both doubles are for a take-out.

One Heart.	Double.	Two Diamonds.	No.
Two Hearts.	No.	No.	Double.

The first double is for a take-out, the second for penalties because West has made a bid.

One Heart.	No.	One No-Trump.	No.
Two Hearts.	Double.		

The double is for penalties, as One Heart could have been doubled for a take-out.

One Heart.	Two Diamonds.	No.	No.
Double.			

The double is for a take-out. A player who has opened the bidding can also make informatory doubles.

Doubling for Penalties

Now that you can distinguish between a double for penalties and a double for a take-out, we can proceed to discuss the requirements for the two types of double. Of penalty doubles it can be said at once that the tendency of all inexperienced players is to double high contracts too often and low contracts not often enough. A moment's calculation will show how heavy the odds are against the doubler on close decisions. Let us say that the opposition are vulnerable and have bid to Four Spades with reasonable confidence. You will have the lead against a Spade contract and your hand is

$$\spadesuit—10\ 5$$
$$\heartsuit—A\ 6\ 3$$
$$\diamondsuit—A\ K\ 6\ 5\ 2$$
$$\clubsuit—K\ Q\ 8$$

You calculate that you will make at least one trick in Hearts, two in Diamonds, and one in Clubs. That looks like one down, and there is always the chance that partner will make a trick as well, and so you double. "Redouble," says the opponent on your left. Partner clenches his teeth, and passes grimly. You consider a flight to Five Diamonds, but reflect that that is sure to be expensive, and anyway they haven't made their contract yet. So you pass and lead the King of Diamonds. Your worst fears are confirmed when dummy goes down with several Spades and no Diamonds at all. The opposition score an overtrick, 480 below and 400 above. Your double has presented them with 730 extra points, the difference between 880 and 150 which they would have scored for Five Spades if the contract had not been doubled. Had you succeeded in defeating them by one trick, your double would have won you only 100 points, the difference between 200 for one down doubled and 100 for one down undoubled.

The following injunction is worth bearing in mind: " Never double an opponent's trump contract on the strength of high cards held by you in side suits. Respect the enemy's intelligence to the point of assuming that the more apparent tricks you hold, the more certain it is that these will not materialise owing to freak distribution. Remember, in general, that mathematically the odds are heavily against the doubler. Remember, also, that your double may help to place the cards and so be the means of presenting the opponents with the opportunity to make their contract."

It is also unwise to double contracts of Three No-Trumps on a strong balanced hand. Your double is sure to assist the declarer in the play of the hand, and you will find that very good-looking hands are worth little when the opposition have all the outstanding strength. Slam contracts, too, should never be doubled on a speculative chance such as an Ace and a King Queen. If the contract is redoubled and made, the trick score for Six of a major suit jumps from 180 to 720, and the chances of profit from the double amount to much less.

Doubles of low contracts at the range of One or Two are much less likely to go astray than doubles of high contracts and they also produce greater penalties. A good time to double is when partner opens the bidding and second hand overcalls in a denomination in which you are strong.

♠—8 4
♡—J 7 6
♢—A Q 6 2
♣—K J 10 8

Suppose that partner opens One Spade and an opponent overcalls with Two Clubs; you could call Two Diamonds with your hand but a much better call is " double." As partner has opened the bidding you may assume that

he has 2½ honour tricks or more.   You have what looks
like three tricks in Clubs, and A Q of Diamonds in
addition.   You are almost sure to defeat the Two Club
contract if it is passed by everyone, and it is quite possible
that if the call was a weak one you will defeat it by three
or four tricks, obtaining a penalty worth more than game.

Many good doubles can be made with less strength in
trumps.

♠—K 8 5 2
♡—9
◇—A 9 3
♣—K 8 6 5 2

Partner opens One Heart and second hand overcalls
"Two Diamonds."   You have a perfectly sound double.
The fact that you have a singleton of your partner's
suit is an excellent recommendation for the double.   You
will lead the singleton and no doubt at some point in the
play you will obtain a Heart ruff.   If by any chance the
opposition were to make Two Diamonds, it would still
not give them game, for twice 40 is only 80.   Had partner's opening bid been One Spade, the double would
have been quite wrong.   In the first place, your defensive possibilities are much smaller when you hold several
cards of partner's suit, for no doubt one or other of the
opposition will be short in the suit, and good cards held
by your side will be wasted.   Secondly, if partner has
bid One Spade, it is very likely that you can go game in
Spades, and you should in fact raise to Three Spades.
But when the opening bid was One Heart, prospects of
game for your side were much less bright.

An intervening bid of One No-Trump by an opponent
is often an easy target for a profitable double.

♠—A J 7
♡—J 10 9 5
◇—K 10 6 2
♣—J 8

Partner opens One Club and an opponent overcalls with One No-Trump. Far and away the best call is to double. It would be particularly foolish to bid Two No-Trumps, contracting to make eight tricks, for if your side can in fact make Two or Three No-Trumps, it follows that you would have been able to defeat the opponent's call of One No-Trump by several tricks.

DOUBLING FOR A TAKE-OUT

Take-out doubles were invented as a solution for the awkward bidding situation in which you have a good hand and want to know where your partner's strength lies.

♠—A 10 8 4
♡—K J 6 3
◇—6
♣—A Q 8 5

You have this hand, and the opponent on your right opens with a bid of One Diamond. If it were not for the informatory double, you would have no good bid to make, for any suit that you chose to bid might be the worst one for your partner. But an informatory double expresses just what you want to convey—that you have a good hand and want to know what is your partner's best suit.

THE DOUBLER'S REQUIREMENTS

The requirements for a take-out double are a minimum of $2\frac{1}{2}$ honour tricks, together with preparedness for any bid that partner may make.

A few examples will make clear the effect of each of these stipulations. In each case the opening bid is One Diamond, and you have to speak as second hand.

♠—Q 10 6 2
♡—K 8 5 4
◇—3
♣—A 10 4 3

This is an admirable holding from the point of view of preparedness, but the high-card strength is too slight for a double; you should pass.

♠—A Q 6 4 2
♡—K J 8 5
◇—7
♣—A 8 3

You might bid One Spade on this hand, but a double is better because partner may hold strength in Hearts and not in Spades.

♠—A 10 7 5 2
♡—K Q 8 5 4
◇— —
♣—K 10 6

A genuine two-suited hand like this is not suitable for a double. You are void in Diamonds, and there is a distinct danger that partner, with strength in Diamonds, will make what is known as a penalty pass. That is to say, he may pass your informatory double, and let the opposition play in One Diamond doubled—a very unsuitable contract for your hand. Your best course is to bid One Spade and hope that you will have an opportunity to bid your Hearts. If you do not bid one of your suits at once, the bidding may well develop in such a way that you never have a chance to show them both.

♠—A J 8
♡—A K J 4 2
◇—A 5 3
♣—10 6

The fact that you hold 4 honour tricks makes a double the best call on this hand. If you bid One Heart or Two Hearts, partner will not appreciate that you hold so many high cards. If you double and bid your Hearts on the next round, he gets a good picture of your holding. A double is generally correct when you hold more than $3\frac{1}{2}$ honour tricks.

♠—Q 8
♡—A 5 3
◇—K J 10 6
♣—A 7 5 2

This time you are very strong in the opponents' suit. The best course is to pass and hope that the opponents get into trouble. If you double and partner bids Spades on a four-card suit, you may get a poor result. A pass may well lead to a good penalty. For example, the opener's partner may respond One No-Trump and this may be passed round to you; now you can double, and if partner has a little strength he will pass the double of One No-Trump, and you are likely to pick up a good penalty. If at any point the opener rebids Two Diamonds, you can double for penalties. It would not be a take-out double because you did not double One Diamond. Remember, then, that if you are strong in the suit opened by the opponents, the best plan is generally to pass and not to double, nor to bid One No-Trump.

A take-out double can be made equally well if both opponents have bid. The bidding may go:

| *South.* | *West.* | *North.* | *East.* |
| One Heart. | No. | Two Clubs. | Double. |

To risk doubling in such a position East should have a good hand such as:

♠—K Q 8 5
♡—A 3
◇—A Q J 2
♣—K 5 4

Note that he is strong in both the unbid suits, one of which he is requesting his partner to show.

The player who has opened the bidding can also make an informatory double:

♠—K J 5 2
♡—8
◇—A Q J 7
♣—A K 6 3

You open One Diamond, and the player on your left bids One Heart. If this is passed by your partner and the next player, you can double, for your hand has support for whatever suit your partner mentions.

PROCEDURE BY THE DOUBLER'S PARTNER

When your partner has made an informatory double he expects you to bid your best suit.

♠—10 7 6 4
♡—5 3
◇—8 6 4 2
♣—Q 8 3

If One Diamond is opened on your left, your partner doubles, and the next hand passes, you must say One Spade. Unless the opponent on your right relieves you of the necessity of bidding by making a call himself, you must never pass just because you are very weak. The only time you can pass is when you have exceptional strength in the suit doubled.

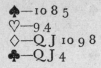

♠—10 8 5
♡—9 4
◇—Q J 10 9 8
♣—Q J 4

With this hand you can pass the double of One Diamond, thus converting the take-out double into a penalty double. You can pass because you are sure to make three or more tricks in defence of One Diamond doubled. When you sit underneath the bidder, you must have a very strong trump holding to make a penalty pass.

♠—Q 8
♡—7 5 4
◇—K J 9 2
♣—10 7 6 4

On this hand you should respond One No-Trump to the double of One Diamond, for your Diamonds are not strong enough for a pass unless you are sitting over the Diamond bidder.

With a fairly good hand containing 2 honour tricks or 1½ honour tricks and a five-card suit, you should make a jump response.

♠—K J 9 5   ♠—K J 8 5 2
♡—A 8   ♡—9
◇—6 4 2   ◇—7 5 4
♣—K 7 5 3   ♣—K Q 8 6

With both these hands you should respond Two Spades to the double of One Diamond so that your partner can tell that although your bid was forced you have fair strength.

A double of One No-Trump can generally be passed.

♠—Q 6 2
♡—K 8 5 3
◇—J 6 2
♣—7 5 4

You should always pass the double of One No-Trump on a balanced hand of this kind with a little strength. You should take out the double if you are weak and have a five-card suit.

♠—Q 6 3
♡—5
◇—9 7 6 4 2
♣—J 6 5 4

On this hand it is plain that you cannot co-operate in the defence to One No-Trump doubled. You should take out into Two Diamonds.

PROCEDURE BY THE OPENER'S PARTNER

If your partner's opening bid is doubled informatorily by second hand, you should act as follows :

If you have a fairly good hand with two honour tricks or more, you should redouble.

If you have a moderate hand with a suit to show, bid the suit as you would have done had there been no double.

If you have a poor hand but support for partner's suit, raise to the limit.

If none of these conditions exists, say " No Bid."

♠—8 4
♡—Q 10 6 3
◇—A Q 5 2
♣—K 9 6

If partner opens One Spade and second hand doubles,

you should redouble.   This tells partner that you have a fair hand, and may well lead to a very profitable penalty double of whatever the opponents call.

♠—K 10 6 4 3
♡—8 2
♢—A 6 4
♣—Q 9 3

If partner's One Heart opening is doubled, make your normal response of One Spade.

♠—Q 10 5 2
♡—8
♢—7 4 3
♣—K 7 6 5 2

If One Spade is doubled, raise to Three Spades with a view to making it difficult for the opposition to get together in Hearts.   The fact that you do not redouble tells partner that you are not really strong, but are jumping to Three Spades for tactical reasons.   Had you held the Ace of Diamonds in addition, you should first have redoubled and later raised the Spades.

S.O.S. Redoubles

There is one more aspect of doubling which must be discussed, and that is the S.O.S. Redouble.   It sometimes happens that a player who has been doubled in a contract of, say, One Diamond may decide that his best chance of escaping a heavy penalty is to force his partner to show his best suit.   The way to do this is to redouble.   The redouble in this case does not signify confidence in your ability to make the contract, but asks for a rescue.   Three conditions must be present if the redouble is to be read as an S.O.S. redouble.   Partner must have passed the doubled contract; partner must have made no bid up to the present; and the contract must be at the range of One or Two.

♠—Q 10 8
♡—K 9 5 2
◇—A Q 6 3
♣—8 4

One Club is opened on your right, and you make a rather doubtful overcall of One Diamond, which is promptly doubled. If the next two players pass, you can redouble, inviting partner to bid Spades or Hearts; in this way you may escape a big penalty.

The redouble for a rescue is most common when a take-out double by second hand has been passed for penalties by fourth hand.

♠—K 10 8 7
♡—8 5
◇—Q 9 3
♣—A K 6 2

You bid One Club and second hand doubles; partner passes and fourth hand passes. You know that there is a strong Club holding on your right and are afraid of playing in One Club doubled. Redouble, and if partner bids One Heart and that is doubled, say One Spade. Do not forget that the redouble is understood to be for a rescue only if partner has already passed the present double. If you open One Diamond, the next two players pass and fourth hand doubles, a redouble by you is a sign of strength.

CHAPTER X

DEFENSIVE AND COMPETITIVE BIDDING

It has been seen that an opening bid of One normally gives promise of a minimum of $2\frac{1}{2}$ honour tricks. For defensive overcalls it is more important to be strong in playing tricks than in honour tricks, which may vary from 1 to $3\frac{1}{2}$. With more than $3\frac{1}{2}$ honour tricks the defender should as a rule double, or, if he has a good suit, make a jump overcall. Many players overcall as a matter of course on hands which do not justify the bid. The examples which follow are worth careful attention.

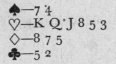

♠—7 4
♡—K Q J 8 5 3
◇—8 7 5
♣—5 2

If the opponent on your right opens One Club, it is reasonable to overcall One Heart on this hand. If you are doubled in one Heart and defeated by three tricks, which is about the worst that can happen, you have the consolation of knowing that you have saved a game or even a slam by the opposing side, so you have not really got a bad result on the hand.

Now let us consider the contrary situation:

♠—A Q 6 4
♡—Q 10 7 5
◇—A 7 3
♣—J 4

This hand is held by West. North opens One Diamond, East passes and South bids One Heart. Now a call of One Spade by West would be atrocious. What does it stand to gain? It can lead to nothing, for both opponents have bid and partner has passed One

Diamond, so that it is extremely unlikely that he has enough to help you make a game. On the other hand, you have excellent values in defence, especially as Hearts have been called on your right, and it is most improbable that the enemy will make a game and very likely that they will get into trouble. Now what does the bid stand to lose? It is not unlikely that you are running into a big double which will give the opponents a fine result on the hand, *because there is no game for them ;* that is the essential difference between this example and the last. If on the previous hand you went down a few hundred in One Heart doubled, you would be sure that you were saving something, but on the present hand that consolation is denied to you if you go down in One Spade doubled.

Perhaps North holds something like:

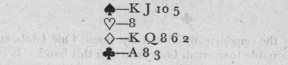

♠—K J 10 5
♡—8
◇—K Q 8 6 2
♣—A 8 3

He will be very quick to double your overcall of One Spade, especially as he has a singleton in the suit which his partner has bid. You have no escape except to One No-Trump, which may be worse, and, as you enter the penalty in the opponents' column, you will have the galling reflection that had you held your peace they would in all probability have failed in whatever contract they reached.

Here are some more examples which illustrate the same principle:

Hand A.	Hand B.	Hand C.
♠—A K 7 6	♠—A Q 7 6 3	♠—K 8 6 4 2
♡—A 4	♡—7 6 5	♡—8 6 4
◇—8 6 5 2	◇—K 5 2	◇—A 6
♣—7 6 3	♣—7 3	♣—5 4 2

None of these hands is a good overcall of an opening One bid, although Hand B might be worth a call non-vulnerable against vulnerable opponents. In every case the overcall of One Spade stands to lose more than it stands to gain.

For an overcall at the range of Two, appreciable extra strength is required, and you must be sure that if you are doubled, the measure of your loss will be the measure of your gain inasmuch as you are preventing the enemy from going game. The following are wicked overcalls of a One Spade bid:

Hand A.	Hand B.	Hand C.
♠—7 6	♠—8 6	♠—Q 10 5 4
♡—A K 7 6 4	♡—A Q J 5	♡—K Q 6 4 3
◇—K 6 4	◇—A 7 6 4	◇—A 5
♣—9 7 6	♣—10 5 2	♣—6 2

Hand A is palpably weak in playing tricks; you might go four or five down to save a game, and that is too high a price to pay. Hand B is too weak for a double, and the Hearts are far too weak for an overcall at the range of Two. On Hand C it would be especially unwise to overcall One Spade with Two Hearts because of your holding in Spades; the enemy probably cannot go far, and Two Hearts doubled may give them a fine result on the hand.

THE JUMP OVERCALL

A jump overcall is the best bid on hands which contain 3 to 4 honour tricks and one strong suit.

♠—8
♡—A K J 10 9 3
◇—A Q 5 2
♣—J 8

Bid Two Hearts over One Club. It would be wrong to double because of the weakness in Spades.

CONTROL-SHOWING OVERCALLS

On hands of an exceptional type an overcall can be made in the opponent's suit. This bid should show first-round control of the suit bid and is forcing to game. It is in effect an exceedingly strong take-out double.

♠—K Q J 5
♡—A Q 10 6 2
◇—   —
♣—A K 7 3

If your opponent opens One Diamond, you can over-call Two Diamonds. Partner responds on the same principles as he would to an informatory double and neither player can drop the bidding short of game. This control-showing overcall should be used very sparingly by the defending side. It can often be used, however, by the side which has opened the bidding.

♠—   —
♡—K 10 6 2
◇—A Q 6 3
♣—K J 8 5 4

Partner opens One Heart and an opponent overcalls One Spade. You bid Two Spades, which at one stroke confirms Heart support, forces to game, and shows first round control of Spades.

The opener can also use this bid.

♠—K Q 8 3
♡—A 5
◇—A K J 6 4 2
♣—Q

This hand is held by South and the bidding goes:

South.	*West.*	*North.*	*East.*
One Diamond.	One Heart.	One Spade.	No bid.

South now bids Two Hearts, forcing to game and showing first round control of Hearts.

DEFENSIVE BIDDING BY FOURTH HAND

If an opening bid is followed by two passes, fourth hand, especially if not strong in the suit opened, can reopen the bidding, either with a double or an overcall, on less than is needed for a bid by second hand.

Hand A.	*Hand B.*
♠—K 5 2	♠—K 8 6 4 2
♡—A 8 5 3	♡—A 10 8 3
◇—10 6	◇—8 5
♣—K Q 4 2	♣—Q 3

An opening bid of One Diamond is followed by two passes. The idea, common to all weak players, that it would be wrong to disturb this innocuous contract, is wholly mistaken; the likelihood is that your side holds the balance of the cards. On Hand A you can reopen with a take-out double. Since the responder passed One Diamond, it is safe to assume that he is very weak, and there is a good chance that partner is lying in wait with a strong hand. On Hand B you can reopen with a bid of One Spade. Were the opening bid One Heart, however, it would be better to pass and let the opponents play in One Heart.

SUPPORTING PARTNER'S OVERCALL

Partner's intervening bids should be supported in much the same way as his opening bids. For a direct raise the necessary trump support is less than is required for the support of an opening bid.   It is unlikely that an overcall is made on a suit of less than five cards, and if it is, there must be compensating values.

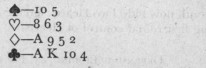

♠—10 5
♡—8 6 3
◇—A 9 5 2
♣—A K 10 4

You are vulnerable and partner has bid Two Hearts over an opening One Spade bid.   To make a vulnerable overcall at the range of Two partner must have a good suit and about six playing tricks.   With three trumps, a doubleton, and three quick tricks, you have excellent support and can raise to Four Hearts.

COMPETITIVE BIDDING

Good judgment in competitive bidding situations comes only with experience and cannot be taught.   It is, however, well to understand the mathematics of such bidding so that you may have some idea of the extent to which it is permissible to overbid in order to prevent the opponents from scoring game.

The value of a non-vulnerable game is between 300 and 350 plus the trick score of 120 or so, altogether about 450.   Therefore, if you are not vulnerable yourself and overbid by two tricks to save the game, you lose 300 for two down doubled, and your bid has shown a profit. If you lose 500 for three down non-vulnerable, or two down vulnerable, your bid shows a small loss.

If the opponents are vulnerable and you are not, the value of the second game to them is about the same, approximately 450.   It is true that if they score game they enter a trick score of 120 odd and a rubber bonus of 700.   This does not mean, however, that the second game has been worth 820 to them, for half the rubber bonus of 700 was in reality won with the first game. Some players find this very difficult to understand, so we will put it another way. If when the opponents are a game up you let them go out with the rubber, they enter a score of 800 or more, but after that you can start a fresh rubber on equal terms with the world. If, on the other hand, when the opponents are a game up you incur a penalty of 500 to save the rubber, you remain with the disadvantage of being still a game down. In actual fact, therefore, it is rather better to lose the rubber than to go down 500 and still be a game down.

If both sides are vulnerable, the value of a game to either side is precisely what is scored, 500 for the rubber plus a trick score of 100 or more. You therefore show a gain if you are two down doubled, losing 500.

The following maxims are sound for competitive bidding:

(1) When in doubt whether to sacrifice or to allow the opponents to have the declaration, sacrifice so long as you are reasonably sure that the opponents can make their contract. Over your sacrifice bid they may call one more and go down. You stand to gain more than you stand to lose.

(2) When in doubt whether to bid one trick more yourself or to double the opponents who are trying to sacrifice, double so long as you are sure that the double will be profitable. Better a certain 300 or more than a problematical 450 which may be minus 100 instead.

(3) When both sides are bidding vigorously, and it seems close whether the enemy will make Four Hearts which they have bid or you will make Four Spades, always bid one more yourself. If you are wrong, your decision will not have cost much; that is to say, if the opponents would have been one down in Four Hearts, and you are one down in Four Spades, you have not lost much. But if they would have made Four Hearts, and you are one down, you have gained appreciably. And

if you make Four Spades, you have gained tremend-ously. Furthermore, there is always the chance that the enemy will misjudge the situation and bid Five Hearts, in the belief—probably mistaken—that you can make Four Spades.

SACRIFICE BIDDING AT A PART SCORE

When the opponents have a part score, beware of the habit, very common amongst all classes of players, of overbidding to a ridiculous extent to prevent them from making game. If the opponents are 60 up, they are already part of the way towards game, so that you should be all the more unwilling to incur a big sacrifice to save it. Yet for some inexplicable reason most players display greater tenacity in contesting a game bid from a part score than a game bid from a love score, despite the fact that the latter is clearly worth the greater sacrifice. The corollary to this is that when you have a part score yourself, you should be all the more ready to double a sacrifice bid by the opponents, so scoring a penalty and retaining the advantage of your part score.

PART III. THE PLAY

CHAPTER XI

THE HANDLING OF SUIT COMBINATIONS

BEFORE you can plan, as declarer, the play of the twenty-six cards before you, you must know how to handle various card combinations to the best advantage. In the first part of this chapter we shall consider how to make the best of various honour combinations, and in the second part we shall discuss the development of low-card tricks.

THE HANDLING OF HONOURS

The first principle to master is that it pays to lead towards honours and not away from them.   Set out the cards in the following way:

A Q

K J   10 9

7 5

If the lead is made by North, he can win a trick with the Ace, but will lose the Queen to West's King. Suppose, however, that South leads the 5; now if West plays the Jack, North covers with the Queen, and, as the cards lie, the Queen wins the trick.   This play is called a finesse.   It is, of course, true that the finesse of the Queen was by no means bound to succeed, for East might have had the King, but even then the finesse would have lost nothing.

K x

x x

In this example it is equally important to lead towards the honour.   If West has the Ace, the King will win a trick.   If the Ace is with East, the King can never win unless East can be made to lead the suit.

(1) A Q J   (2) K Q x

x x x   x x x

With the first holding a finesse against the King can be taken twice, provided that the lead is made on each occasion from South.   All three tricks can be won if West has the King.   In the second example, it can be every bit as important to lead twice up to the K Q x, because if the Ace is with West, he cannot prevent your

making two tricks, but if you lead the King or Queen
from dummy (assuming North is dummy), West will fell
it with his Ace and you will make only one trick.

(1) A x   (2) A J
    Q J   Q x

These combinations show two more ways in which a
finesse can be taken against a King, and you will understand by now how to do this by leading from the South
hand. It is important to note that if you add a small
card to each hand in the latter combination, the
finesse no longer wins an extra trick.

(1)   A x x

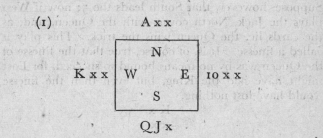

K x x   W   E   10 x x

                       Q J x

(2)   A J x

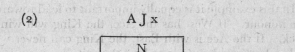

K 10 x   W   E   9 x x

                       Q x x

In the first example you can lead the Queen and run
it, if not covered. When you follow with the Jack,
West is sure to cover. Whether he covers on the first
round or the second, you can win only two tricks, and

these you would have won equally by straightforward play of the Ace followed by a lead to the Q J.

In the second example the same situation exists; you can lead a small card and finesse the Jack, but if on the next round you lead the Queen, West will cover and the opponents will win the third round. Had your side held the 10 in either of these examples, the finesse would have won a trick.

(1) A 10 x   (2) A J x
    Q J x   Q 10 x

Now if West has the King, it is trapped, and North-South can win all three tricks.

In certain circumstances an attempt to finesse can actually lose a trick. Consider this situation:

A x x
Q x x

Now the lead of the Queen by South in a misguided attempt to finesse can well lose a trick. If West has the King, he can play it on the Queen, so that whatever happens only the Ace is made. But by playing from dummy towards the Queen, a second trick can be made if East has the King.

FINESSING AGAINST A QUEEN

The examples so far have been of finesses against a King. Finesses against a Queen are equally common.

K J x x
A x x x

South should play the Ace and then lead a small card with a view to finessing the Jack if the Queen has not been played. The point of playing the Ace first is that

East may have a singleton Queen. If you take a first-round finesse of the Jack and lose to a singleton Queen, it will cost you a trick which could have been saved by playing the Ace first.

A 10 x
K J x

This combination has an interesting feature in that a finesse can be taken against either opponent. If you think that West has the Queen, you can play the King and then lead towards the Ace 10. If you place the Queen with East, you play the Ace first and then finesse the Jack.

A K x x

	N	
Q x	W E	10 x x
	S	

J x x x

This situation is analogous to the one we gave above of A x x facing Q x x. No finesse is playable. If the Jack is led, the Queen covers, and the third round is won by East's 10. The correct play is to lead the Ace and King in the hope of the Queen falling in two rounds.

(1) K J 10   (2) K 10 9
   x x x   J x x

In these examples both the Ace and Queen are missing, but a finesse is playable against the Queen. In the first example a small card is led, and if West plays low the 10 is finessed; if this card holds the trick, or if it fetches the Ace from East, the lead towards the King Jack is repeated. Note that this method of handling the

suit does not cost a trick if West has the Ace and East
the Queen. If that is the position, it is true that you
can win the first trick by going up with the King, but you
will lose the next one, and the K J 10 are good for one
trick however you play them.

In the second example a finesse against the Queen
stands to win in much the same way. Note that when
the King Jack and 10 are not all in the same hand, the
9 is needed in one hand or the other in order to
make the finesse a profitable venture. For if the distribution is:

K 10 x

Q x x | N | A 9 x

     W   E

     S

J x x

the defence can win two tricks by covering the Jack with
the Queen.

FINESSES AGAINST THE JACK AND TEN

If your side holds the Ace, King, and Queen, it is
seldom that a finesse against the Jack will be the right
play.

A Q 10 x
K x x

With this holding you should start off by playing a small
card to the Ace, back to the King, and then a small
card to the Q 10. If West follows with a small card and
the Jack has not yet been played, you have the choice of
finessing the 10, or playing the Queen and hoping that
the Jack will drop from East. There is only one card

outstanding, and mathematically the play for the drop is slightly superior, but conditions in actual play may point to the finesse.

K x x
Q 10 x

This is the commonest example of a finesse against the Jack. A small card is led to the King, and whether or not East wins with the Ace, the 10 is finessed on the next round. So, irrespective of the position of the Ace, two tricks are made if East has the Jack; note that if you can induce West to open up this suit, you are assured of two tricks however the cards lie.

Q x x
J 9 x

This time you finesse against the 10. Play small to the Queen; unless West holds both top honours, East will win with the Ace or King. When next in dummy, lead small towards the Jack 9 and finesse the 9, hoping to force the other top honour from West. It is true that if East has both Ace and King it is better to put up the Jack on the second round, but the finesse against the 10 is the better chance in the long run. Note again that if either opponent opens this suit, you are assured of one trick, as you will not play an honour to the first lead (except to win it) and will therefore be able to make a trick with the Queen or Jack on the third round.

DOUBLE AND COMBINATION FINESSES

The examples given so far have all been of finesses taken against one card, the adjacent cards in the suit being held by the finessing side. If a player has to attack a suit in which the opponents hold several honours, he may have to take a double or combination

finesse. The simplest example of a double finesse is
seen in this situation:

A Q 10

x x x

If South held the Jack, he would merely have to take
a simple finesse against the King. As it is, he has to
try to make the greatest number of tricks while the
opponents hold the King and Jack. If both these cards
lie in East's hand, then only the Ace can be made, unless
East can be forced to lead the suit. If the honours are
split—one with East and one with West—two tricks can
be made whether the Queen or 10 is finessed on the first
round, but if both honours lie with West, all three tricks
can be made provided that the 10 is finessed on the first
round. If the Queen is played on the first round, West
will make the King or Jack. But if the 10 is finessed and
holds, South can lead again from his own hand and
finesse the Queen, losing no tricks at all. The correct
play, therefore, is to finesse the 10 on the first round, and,
if this holds, the Queen on the second.

The position is essentially the same if the distribution
is:

K J x

x x x

The lower honour—the Jack—should be finessed on the
first round so that two tricks can be made if West has
both Ace and Queen.

A J 10

Q x x   N
       W   E   K x x
         S

x x x

A holding of this kind is said to present a combination finesse. Unless East has both King and Queen, two tricks can be made by correct play. A small card is led, and if West plays low the 10 is finessed. If this loses to the King or Queen, a second lead is made towards the Ace Jack and a finesse taken against the other honour.

A 10 x
J 9 x

This situation is in effect the same as the last. A finesse is taken on the first round, to be followed by a second finesse against the outstanding honour.

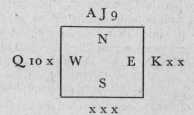

If the cards lie favourably, two tricks can be made with A J 9, opposite x x x. A small card is led and the 9 finessed; if this forces the King or Queen from East, a second finesse can be taken. It is true that if the distribution had been

A J 9

K Q x   W   E   10 x x

x x x

a first-round finesse of the Jack would have been the winning play, but the finesse of the 9, which stood to win two tricks if West had K 10 or Q 10, offered the superior chance.

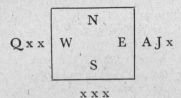

K 10 9 x

Q x x W N E A J x
         S

x x x

The play with this combination is to finesse the 9 on the first round. If this loses to the Jack or Queen, a second finesse of the 10 should be taken.

PROMOTION OF LOW-CARD TRICKS

We have been concerned so far with the best method of handling honour combinations. Equally important is the development of low-card winners. Consider this simple combination:

K Q x x
A x x

It is obvious that you can win three tricks by virtue of the three top honours. What chance do you think you have of winning a fourth trick? If you are a complete beginner, you will have to make a calculation along these lines:—" Between the dummy and yourself you hold seven cards and the opponents therefore hold six. You can win three rounds with Ace, King, and Queen. If the opponents' cards are divided 3-3, they will have to follow to all three rounds, and the fourth round in dummy will then be the master." With very little experience, however, you will recognise at a glance that you had a chance of developing the fourth winner if the opposition cards are equally divided.

K Q x x
A x x x

This time you again hold the three top honours, but you have eight cards of the suit. So long as the opponents' cards are divided 3–2 and not 4–1 or 5–0, you will win the fourth round of the suit, as well as the first three. Your chance of developing the low-card winner is much better than in the last example, when you needed to find six cards breaking exactly 3–3. It is worth knowing that the odds strongly favour a 3–2 division of five outstanding cards, but the odds are against a 3–3 break of six outstanding cards.

A J x x

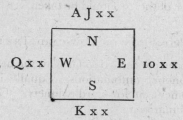

Q x x　|　W　　　E　|　10 x x

K x x

With this distribution you can win one additional high-card trick by means of a finesse against the Queen, and one low-card trick by virtue of the 3–3 break. You play the King and then finesse the Jack: this wins and you lay down the Ace. When both opponents follow to this third round, you know that dummy's fourth card is a winner.

A x x x

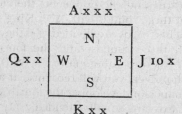

Q x x　|　W　　　E　|　J 10 x

K x x

In this example we encounter a new principle. One trick must be lost, and it is as well to lose it on the first round. So a small card is led and a small card is also played from dummy. The opponents win, but the three remaining tricks can all be won by declarer, thanks to the 3–3 break. The low play from each hand on the first lead is known as " ducking."

A K x x x

```
        +-----------+
        |     N     |
Q x x   |  W     E  |   J 10
        |     S     |
        +-----------+
```

x x x

The same play is made with this holding: one trick must be lost, and it is given up at once. Then the remaining four cards in dummy are all winners.

A Q x x x

```
        +-----------+
        |     N     |
K J x   |  W     E  |   10 x x
        |     S     |
        +-----------+
```

x x

This time declarer ducks on the first round and finesses on the second. The distribution of the opposing cards is so favourable that four tricks can be won.

We now come to some rather less simple combinations, in which the right play is not obvious.

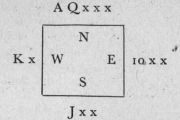

A Q x x x

K x   W   E   10 x x

J x x

This combination is one which players even of some experience often play wrongly. It is a mistake to lead the Jack, because if it is covered the opponents are bound to win the third round. The low card should be led and the Queen finessed. If it holds, the Ace should be laid down. Then, as West had K x, the King falls and all five tricks can be won. You will find that an original lead of the Jack cannot possibly gain.

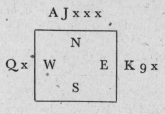

A J x x x

Q x   W   E   K 9 x

10 x x

If the 9 had been held in either hand, the right play would have been to take two finesses as shown above. Lacking the 9, declarer's best chance of making four tricks is to lead a small card and play the Jack from dummy. This will probably lose to the King or Queen, and on the next round the Ace is laid down. If this brings down the other honour from West, all the remaining tricks can be made. Note that an original lead of the 10 does not avail to win four tricks, for West will

cover the honour, and then East wins with the King and
the 9.

J x x
A K x x

The best way to develop three tricks from this combination is actually to play the Ace and then lead low
towards the J x. If the opposing cards are distributed
3–3, the long card can be made however the suit is
tackled. The advantage of leading towards the J x is
that in this way the Jack wins if West has four cards
headed by the Queen. For if the distribution is:

J x x

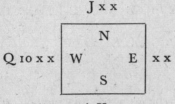

Q 10 x x   W   N   E   x x
     S

A K x x

only the Ace and King will be made if these cards are
played out at once. But if on the first or second round a
small card is led to the Jack, West will make only his
Queen. It is true that if East had had originally Q x,
this method of play would not be as successful as
playing out Ace and King, but the distribution in which
West has four cards headed by the Queen and East a
low doubleton is more probable than that in which West
has four cards without the Queen.

K x x x
Q x x x

This combination calls for a type of play different
from anything that we have considered so far. In

certain circumstances three tricks can be won. If it is thought that West is as likely to hold the Ace as East, the first play should be a small card towards the King. If this holds the trick, it is reasonable to assume that the Ace is with West. Declarer should play a small card back and play low from his own hand. He cannot possibly gain by putting the Queen on, and should place West with the Ace alone. If the original distribution was:

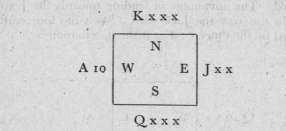

K x x x

A 10   N / W   E / S   J x x

Q x x x

three tricks can be won by this method of play. It should be noted that if East has the Ace, three tricks can be made only if the first lead is made from dummy and if East has a doubleton.

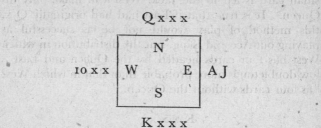

Q x x x

10 x x   N / W   E / S   A J

K x x x

If this is the distribution, three tricks can be won only if the first lead is made from North.

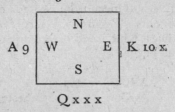

A similar type of play—sometimes called an obligatory finesse—can be made with this combination. A small card is led to the Jack and the trick is won by East's King. On the next round declarer plays low from each hand, his best chance being to find the remaining high honour single with West.

❧

CHAPTER XII

THE PLAY AT NO-TRUMPS

THE play at No-Trumps generally develops into a struggle between the opposing sides to establish their respective long suits. It is the object of the defenders to establish their own long suits before the declarer can establish his. For this reason the player in the lead should normally open his longest suit.

THE LEAD FROM A LONG SUIT

Convention demands that unless three honours are held in the suit, the fourth best should be led. Thus from a holding such as K 7 6 4 3, the proper lead is the 4. With certain honour combinations a high card should be led and not the fourth best. The general rule—as will be seen from the table which follows—is to lead the top of a sequence (Queen from Q J 10) or the higher of touching honours (Jack from A J 10), an exception to this being that a King is led before an Ace.

From a suit headed by:

A K Q	lead	K
A K	„	4th best
A K J	„	K
A Q J	„	Q
A J 10	„	J
K Q J	„	K
K Q 10	„	K
K J 10	„	J
Q J 10	„	Q
Q J 9	„	Q
J 10 9	„	J
J 10 8	„	J
A 10 9	„	10
K 10 9	„	10
Q 10 9	„	10

From all other combinations lead the fourth best. It is important to understand the necessity for leading the small card and not the King from a long suit headed by the Ace King. The lead of the King enables the player to hold the trick and to see the dummy for what that is worth, but the distribution may well be:

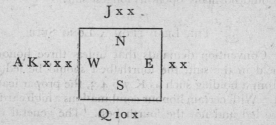

J x x

N
A K x x x W   E x x
S

Q 10 x

Now the defender can clear the suit in three rounds by leading the King, Ace, and a small one, but the disadvantage of this is that if partner later obtains the lead, he has none of the suit to play, and unless the original leader has a quick entry, the remaining winners are wasted. Had the opening lead been a small card, however, the partner of the opening leader would still have had a card to lead back.

THE LEAD FROM A SHORT SUIT

If an opponent has bid the leader's best suit, or if the lead from his longest suit appears particularly unattractive, as it might from such a holding as A Q x x, the best alternative is the highest card from three small ones (the 8 from 8 6 2) or the higher card from a doubleton (the 8 from 8 4). The fact that so high a card as the 8 has been led will generally make it clear to partner that the lead is from " top of nothing," and not the fourth best.

♠—Q 10 7 6 3
♡—8 5
♢—7 6 4
♣—A K 4

The lead against a No-Trump contract should be the ♠ 6; if the opponents have bid Spades, the ♢ 7 is the best choice. A bad lead in either case would be the ♣ King. It is a mistake to release controls in short suits which may well be needed to provide entry for the establishment of your long suits.

♠—K Q 6 4
♡—10 9 5
♢—J 9 5 3
♣—6 4

The lead away from the K Q of Spades is unattractive, as it is all too likely to give the opponents a cheap trick with the Jack. The ◇ 3 may well be better, and many players would prefer the ♡ 10 to either lead. The full bidding must be known before it can be said that any one of these leads is better than another.

♠—8
♡—Q 6 5 4 2
◇—K Q J 9
♣—10 5 4

The strong sequence in Diamonds makes the ◇ King both a safer and a more powerful lead than the ♡ 4.

THE LEAD WHEN PARTNER HAS BID

If partner has bid a suit and the opponents have contracted for No-Trumps over it, you should lead his suit, unless your own hand presents a particularly good alternative. You should lead the highest card from three small ones, and the higher from a doubleton. From four or more cards, always lead the fourth best. Partner will not assume this card to be your highest unless he is a beginner. Suppose, for example, that North bids One Diamond, East One Heart, South One No-Trump, and North Three No-Trumps. The distribution of Hearts is:

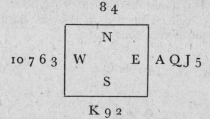

8 4

10 7 6 3   W | E   A Q J 5

K 9 2

Now on the lead of the 3, partner should not imagine that you have the singleton 3, or 3 2 alone, for if you had this would place declarer with K 10 9 7 6, and if that had been his holding no doubt he would have made a penalty double when the intervening call of One Heart was made.

The lowest card should also be led from a holding of three cards headed by Ace, King, Queen, or Jack. The object of this is to make the best use of the honour held by the leader. The distribution may be:

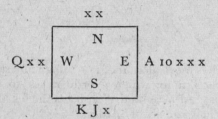

If West leads the Queen, declarer makes two tricks, but only one trick if West leads small and East plays the Ace. It is true that it is not always possible for the leader's partner to judge whether the lead is from four small, three to an honour, or four to an honour, but this uncertainty is generally resolved on the next round.

HOLD-UP PLAY

It was remarked at the beginning of this chapter that the play at a No-Trump contract generally developed into a struggle between the two sides to establish their long suits. The principal device available to the declarer to prevent the establishment of an opponent's long suit is hold-up play, which consists of the retention of a controlling card until one of the opponents is void in the suit. The following hand illustrates the use of this very common play:

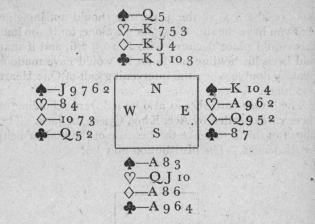

South is the dealer, and, not being vulnerable, he bids One No-Trump, which North raises to Three No-Trumps. All pass, and West leads the fourth best of his longest suit, the Six of Spades.

Trick 1: West leads ♠ 6, North plays ♠ Q, East plays ♠ K, South plays ♠ 3.

Declarer was quite right to put up the Queen of Spades, for had West held the King, the Queen would have won, and it would have been fatal not to play it. As the cards lie, it makes no difference whether the Queen is played or not, for if the 5 is played, East should finesse the 10, retaining his King to catch the Queen in dummy. By so doing East might, for all he knows, be allowing South to win the trick with the Jack, but if South has the Jack, he has a stop in the suit however East plays, so the finesse of the 10 does no harm.

When the Queen is played and covered with the King, South realises that he can never make more than one trick in the suit. This being so, his right play is to withhold his Ace until the third round, the purpose of this being to exhaust one opponent of Spades. The value of this hold-up play will become clear later on.

Trick 2: East leads ♠ 10, South plays ♠ 8, West plays ♠ 2, North plays ♠ 5.

East naturally returns his partner's suit, for no other attack looks promising. It is worth remarking that when West plays the ♠ 2, it is clear to all the players that he held at least five of the suit originally, for his original lead of the 6 was presumably his fourth best, and as he now produces a lower card, that must be his fifth or sixth best.

Trick 3: East plays ♠ 4, South plays ♠ A, West plays ♠ 7, North plays ♣ 3.

Trick 4: South leads ♡ Q, West plays ♡ 4, North plays ♡ 3, East plays ♡ 2.

As South cannot go game without setting up tricks in Hearts—for at the best he could make only one Spade, three Diamonds, and four Clubs—he therefore attacks Hearts, hoping that West, whom he places with two winning Spades, does not hold the Ace of Hearts. It makes no difference whether East wins this trick in Hearts or a later one.

Trick 5: South leads ♡ J, West plays ♡ 8, North plays ♡ 5, East plays ♡ A.

It is at this point in the hand that the object of declarer's hold-up play appears. *East has no Spade to lead to his partner*, and a Heart lead is as good as anything.

Trick 6: East leads ♡ 6, South plays ♡ 10, West plays ◇ 3, North plays ♡ 7.

South can see eight tricks, a Spade, three Hearts, two Diamonds and two Clubs. To develop his ninth he takes a finesse against West, as he does not mind letting East into the lead.

Trick 7: South leads ♣ 4, West plays ♣ 2, North plays ♣ 10, East plays ♣ 7.

As it happens, the finesse wins, and South can now make all the remaining tricks, for the Clubs are good, and the King of Hearts gives a discard for the losing Diamond. South therefore makes Four No-Trumps.

When not to Hold Up

There are many combinations of cards where hold-up play must be wrong because it sacrifices the second stopper. Consider this distribution:

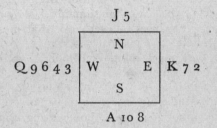

West leads the 4, North plays the 5 (it would be fatal to put on the Jack), and East plays the King. Now it would be very misguided to hold up the Ace. So long as the Ace is played, declarer is assured of a second stopper, for the Jack and 10 are equals against the Queen.

A similar situation is the following:

10 8 4 3

K Q 6 5 2   W   N   E   J 7

S

A 9

The 5 is led, the 3 is played from dummy, and East plays the Jack. You must win with the Ace, for the 10 9 8 must then provide a second trick.

Hold-up play is often wrong on tactical grounds. It is wrong to hold up when a switch by the opposition would be more devastating than a continuation of the suit led.

North

♠—A 6 2
♡—J 7 3
♢—K Q 10 9 8
♣—Q 4

♠ 3 led.

South

♠—J 8 4
♡—A 5 4
♢—J 7 3
♣—A K 8 6

South bids One Club, North responds One Diamond, and South makes a minimum rebid of One No-Trump. With a five-card suit and a fair hand, North should raise to Three No-Trumps. The opposing hands are not given, as it is important that you should appreciate the proper play by the declarer without seeing them. The opening lead by West is the ♠ 3. The first point that South should note is that the 3 has been led and the 2 is in dummy. This means that if West has led the conventional fourth best, he cannot have more than four of the suit. If declarer plays low from dummy, East may win and, having made the same deduction regarding the length of West's holding, switch to Hearts. In this way the defence, when they win with the ♢ A, may altogether take three tricks in Hearts, one in Spades, and one in Diamonds, thus defeating the contract. Declarer's right play therefore is to win the opening lead with the Ace. He then forces out the ♢ A, and the defence take three tricks in Spades, but that is the limit of their success.

It might be concluded from the play of this hand that the convention of leading fourth best assists the declarer more than the defenders. Experience has shown, however, that it is more important to inform partner than to misinform the declarer, and as a matter of fact, even if the lead on this hand had been the ♠ 5, in which case it would have been uncertain whether West had four or five Spades, the Ace would still have been the correct play from dummy.

DUCKING AND SUIT-ESTABLISHMENT PLAY

The main problem in the declarer's play which has so far been dealt with is that of preventing the opponents from establishing their long suits, and it has been shown that this is done by holding up master cards until one of the enemy is exhausted of the suit in question. We now come to consider the equally important matter of establishing the declarer's own long suits. In the examples given so far, there has been no difficulty in doing this ; all the declarer has had to do has been to force out the opponents' stopper and then his suit has been good. Very often it is not as simple as this, and the declarer has to resort to some device, much the most frequent being ducking play.

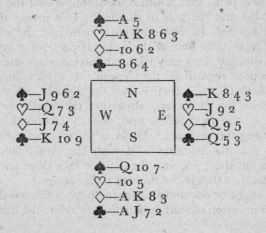

```
                  ♠—A 5
                  ♡—A K 8 6 3
                  ◇—10 6 2
                  ♣—8 6 4

  ♠—J 9 6 2        N         ♠—K 8 4 3
  ♡—Q 7 3                    ♡—J 9 2
  ◇—J 7 4     W         E    ◇—Q 9 5
  ♣—K 10 9        S         ♣—Q 5 3

                  ♠—Q 10 7
                  ♡—10 5
                  ◇—A K 8 3
                  ♣—A J 7 2
```

South bids One Diamond and North responds One Heart. South might now bid his second suit, Clubs, but on the whole his best rebid is One No-Trump, which shows that his hand is not very strong and is of even pattern. North is worth another bid, and being rather strong for the weak bid of Two Hearts he should bid Two No-Trumps. It is close whether South should bid the game, but he can just do so, as he has already told his partner that his hand is not far from a minimum. Against Three No-Trumps West leads ♠ 2.

Trick 1 : West leads ♠ 2, North plays ♠ 5, East plays ♠ K, South plays ♠ 7.

It would be bad play on South's part to put up the Ace from dummy; by playing low he makes sure of two tricks in the suit whoever has the King.

Trick 2: East leads ♠ 3, South plays ♠ 10, West plays ♠ 6, North plays ♠ Ace.

East has a strong holding of his partner's suit and has no reason not to return it. He chooses the 3—his original fourth best. This is the correct play when four or more cards of partner's suit are held. Partner should not be misled into thinking that the 3 is East's only Spade, for declarer can hardly have had five Spades originally.

Counting up his tricks South can see on top two Spades, two Diamonds, and one Club—seven tricks in all. The best chance of establishing the two low-card tricks necessary for contract lies in finding a 3–3 Heart split.

Trick 3: North leads ♡ 3, East plays ♡ 2, South plays ♡ 10, West plays ♡ Q.

In leading a low card from dummy, South is making use of ducking play. He knows that the defenders must make at least one trick in Hearts. If the Ace, King, and a small Heart are played out the suit may be established, but there will be no entry to North's hand to make the two long Hearts.

It makes no difference how the defenders play from this point. Knowing that South has the ♠ Q (for with K Q East would have played the Q on the first trick), and judging that the Hearts are established winners, West may try the lead of the ♣ 10 in the vain hope of making some quick winners in this suit. Whatever West leads, however, declarer can win the trick, lead a heart to Dummy, and go game with at least two tricks in Spades, four in Hearts, two in Diamonds, and one in Clubs.

SUIT ESTABLISHMENT BY THE DEFENDERS

In the play of the next hand it is the defenders who make use of ducking play to establish their long cards.

<pre>
                    ♠—K J 10
                    ♡—9 5 3
                    ◇—Q J 9 4
                    ♣—K J 2

    ♠—A 6 5 3   N   ♠—Q 8 2
    ♡—J 6 2   ♡—A Q 8 4
    ◇—K 3 2   W   E   ◇—7 6
    ♣—9 7 6   S   ♣—10 8 5 4

                    ♠—9 7 4
                    ♡—K 10 7
                    ◇—A 10 8 5
                    ♣—A Q 3
</pre>

South, non-vulnerable, bids One No-Trump, which North raises to Two No-Trumps. Having a somewhat minimum hand, South does not bid game, so the contract remains at Two No-Trumps.

Trick 1: West leads ♠ 3, North plays ♠ 10, East plays ♠ Q, South plays ♠ 4.

The play of the 10 from dummy is naturally correct, for in this way declarer can make two tricks in the suit if West has the Queen. On the play of the 10 East should not be so mean as to withhold his Queen for fear that it may be taken by the Ace. If South has the Ace, he is assured of three tricks anyway, but if he has not the Ace, then it is fatal for East not to put on his Queen.

Trick 2: East leads ♡ 4, South plays ♡ 7, West plays ♡ J, North plays ♡ 3.

East's decision to lead a Heart instead of a Spade is perfectly correct. He noted that his partner led the 3 of Spades and he holds the 2 himself. He concludes from this that partner holds only four Spades, so by continuing Spades only one extra trick is established for the defence. It is therefore best to attack at another point. Hearts are the obvious choice, and the fourth best should be led.

South was right to play low. He cannot gain by putting on the King of Hearts, and there is a possibility that East has led from Q J x x, in which case West will have to put the Ace on to win the trick.

Trick 3: West leads ♡ 6, North plays ♡ 5, East plays ♡ 8, South plays ♡ 10.

Since his partner returned a low Heart, West places him with at least four in the suit, so he continues this line of defence. If West had not known that East held length in Hearts, he would probably have tried a lead through dummy's Clubs. East played well in not putting on his Ace of Hearts. He places West with a third Heart, and wishes to leave him with a Heart to lead to the A Q. It is clear from the play that South has the King of Hearts, for West would have played the King had he held it.

Trick 4: South leads ♣ 3, West plays ♣ 6, North plays ♣ J, East plays ♣ 4.

South enters dummy in order to take the Diamond finesse.

Trick 5: North leads ◇ Q, East plays ◇ 6, South plays ◇ 5, West plays ◇ K.

Trick 6: West leads ♡ 2, North plays ♡ 9, East plays ♡ A, South plays ♡ K.

The value of East's ducking play is now apparent. He wins the next trick with the Queen of Hearts, and then plays a Spade to his partner's Ace. The defenders have won two tricks in Spades, three in Hearts, and one in Diamonds—six in all—so that the contract is defeated by one trick. The contract could, as a matter of fact, still have been defeated had East returned a Spade at trick 2, provided that West won with the Ace and immediately switched to Hearts. The play for the defence was made much easier, however, through East playing Hearts at the second trick. Another way of defeating the contract would have been for the defenders, after they had won a trick with the Jack of Hearts, to clear the thirteenth Spade. The one fatal course of action would have been the unimaginative play of three rounds of Spades at the beginning, for declarer could then have taken the Diamond finesse, and after that he would have lost only the thirteenth Spade and the Ace of Hearts.

❧

CHAPTER XIII

THE PLAY AT SUIT CONTRACTS

THE OPENING LEAD

DISCUSSING the opening lead at No-Trump contracts we found that the importance of the time element was such that it is generally correct for the defender to lead his longest suit. Such tactics are not so effective at a trump contract, however, because as a rule the declarer can stop the run of your long suit by ruffing it. Sometimes a defender by repeatedly forcing declarer to ruff can reduce him to a point at which he is unable to draw the trumps against him. Only when that happens does any direct advantage arise from the lead of a long suit.

It must not be thought from this, however, that it is in any sense bad play to lead a suit which declarer can ruff. Even if it does not cause him eventually to lose control of the trump situation, the lead has done no harm and conforms to the requirement of safety which in the majority of cases decides the choice of lead to a suit contract. A lead from a strong sequence such as K Q J or Q J 10 has the advantage of being both safe and constructive. As at No-Trumps the top of the sequence should be led. From a suit headed by A K or A K Q the King should be led. When no such strong honour combination is held it is generally better to lead from a suit with no honours than from a single honour or two broken honours.

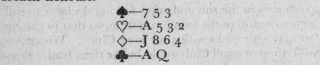

♠—7 5 3
♡—A 5 3 2
♢—J 8 6 4
♣—A Q

The seven of Spades is probably the best lead to any suit contract, including Spades. The lead of a trump is often made with a special purpose, that of preventing declarer from making separately his own and dummy's trumps. In this instance we suggest the lead of the Spade because it is less likely to give a trick away than any other lead. If a Diamond were led from this hand, fourth best would be correct; if a Heart, the Ace, for it is dangerous to underlead Aces against suit contracts, although we do not say that it should never be done.

LEADING FROM A SHORT SUIT

There is one class of lead which has no parallel at No-Trumps, and that is the lead from a singleton or doubleton made in the hope of obtaining a ruff.

♠—K 10 6 4
♡—A 5 3
◇—2
♣—Q J 8 5 2

Against a Heart contract, ◇ 2 is a promising lead because there are two chances of obtaining a ruff; not only may partner have the Ace, but also there is a good chance that after winning the first or second round of trumps you can put him in with Spades or Clubs to give you a Diamond ruff. Against a Spade contract, curiously enough, the lead of the singleton Diamond is not necessarily good. You should realise that your Spades are almost certain to win two tricks in any event. To use them in ruffing Diamonds simply weakens your prospects of defeating the hand. A stronger defence is to attack with Clubs, hoping to set up winners in the suit and, after forcing declarer to ruff, to gain control of the trump situation, so that in the end you may win tricks with your long Clubs. Whereas at No-Trumps a small Club would be the right lead, against a suit contract the Queen is better.

The lead of a doubleton is less likely to produce a ruff than the lead of a singleton, but nevertheless it is a fairly safe lead, and should generally be preferred to the lead from a broken honour combination. It is not as a rule good to lead from A x, K x, Q x, or J x, for such leads are all too likely to lose a trick. Nevertheless the first two can sometimes be tried as desperation measures.

THE PROBLEM OF DRAWING TRUMPS

The declarer at a suit contract is always faced, as soon as he has the lead, with the problem of whether or not to lead trumps. Trumps should always be drawn unless there is a clearly defined reason why trump leads should be postponed.

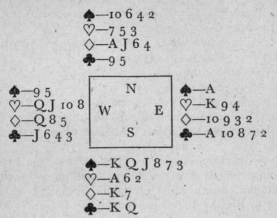

♠—10 6 4 2
♡—7 5 3
◇—A J 6 4
♣—9 5

♠—9 5
♡—Q J 10 8
◇—Q 8 5
♣—J 6 4 3

♠—A
♡—K 9 4
◇—10 9 3 2
♣—A 10 8 7 2

♠—K Q J 8 7 3
♡—A 6 2
◇—K 7
♣—K Q

South opens with One Spade and North gives him a simple raise to Two Spades; East cannot venture a bid at the level of Three, so he passes and South bids Four Spades.

Trick 1: West leads ♡ Q, North plays ♡ 3, East plays ♡ 9, South plays ♡ 2.

West naturally chooses for his lead the top of a strong sequence, and East plays the 9, an unnecessarily high card, as a sign of encouragement to his partner. Had he had K x only, he would have played the King on his partner's Queen so as not to stop the run of the suit. South's play in refusing to win this trick is not as important as it would have been at No-Trumps; it stands to gain only if one opponent has a doubleton Heart and both the black Aces, for then the other opponent may never get in to make the third Heart.

Trick 2: West leads ♡ J, North plays ♡ 5, East plays ♡ 4, South plays ♡ A.

Declarer now reviews his prospects and sees that he is in danger of losing one Spade, two Hearts, and one Club. In fact if he clears trumps at once this is sure to happen. There is a chance, however, that a discard of a Heart can be obtained after a successful finesse in Diamonds.

Trick 3: South leads ♢ K, West plays ♢ 5, North plays ♢ 4, East plays ♢ 2.

Trick 4: South leads ♢ 7, West plays ♢ 8, North plays ♢ J, East plays ♢ 3.

So far so good.   Now so long as the Ace of Diamonds is not ruffed, South can discard his losing Heart.

Trick 5: North leads ♢ A, East plays ♢ 9, South plays ♡ 6, West plays ♢ Q.

Now declarer is home. He plays a Spade from dummy which East wins. If East plays his fourth Diamond, South must be careful to trump with the Jack so that West has no chance to over-ruff with the Nine.

One further lesson from this hand is that one must always play with an eye on the contract. It may have struck you that had the finesse in Diamonds gone wrong South would have been two down on his contract, one more than was at any time necessary. That is true, but of course the risk was nothing to set against the chance of making the contract. Had the contract been Three Spades, on the other hand, it would have been very bad play to take the finesse in Diamonds. The trumps should have been drawn at once and four tricks conceded.

In the next hand declarer does not draw trumps immediately because he wants to use dummy's trumps for ruffing. The hand also shows that what is bad policy for the declarer is good policy for the defenders.

The contract is Four Hearts by South and West leads ♣ K.   Remember that from holdings headed by the A K, the King is led and not the usual top of a sequence.

Trick 1: West leads ♣ K, North plays ♣ 2, East plays ♣ 8, South plays ♣ 4.

East's play of the 8 is the commencement of what is known as a " peter."   The play of a higher followed by

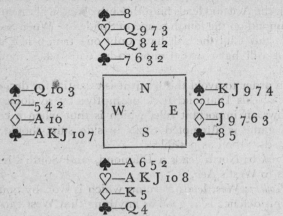

♠—8
♡—Q 9 7 3
◇—Q 8 4 2
♣—7 6 3 2

♠—Q 10 3   N   ♠—K J 9 7 4
♡—5 4 2   W   E   ♡—6
◇—A 10   ◇—J 9 7 6 3
♣—A K J 10 7   S   ♣—8 5

♠—A 6 5 2
♡—A K J 10 8
◇—K 5
♣—Q 4

a lower card at a suit contract shows either strength in the suit or a doubleton. The signal to partner is very often of the greatest importance.

Trick 2: West leads ♣ A, North plays ♣ 3, East plays ♣ 5, South plays ♣ Q.

Without much thought West pursues what seems to him to be a fairly safe defence.

Trick 3: West leads ♣ Jack, North plays ♣ 6, East discards ♠ 4, South trumps with ♡ 8.

Now it should be evident to declarer that he needs dummy's trumps for Spade ruffs. To draw trumps would be fatal.

Trick 4: South leads ♠ A and all follow.

Trick 5: South leads a small Spade and trumps in dummy.

At this point declarer has to be careful about the order of play. Naturally he wants to ruff two more losing Spades, and he could do this by re-entering his hand first with a lead of trumps and then by ruffing the fourth Club. This line of play loses, however, owing to the 3—1 break in trumps. After the fourth Spade has been ruffed, declarer leads a Diamond from North, West wins with the Ace and leads his fifth Club (West will discard a Diamond on the fourth round of Spades). When South ruffs this Club he will have only one trump left, and West will have two trumps, so he will make another trick.

In order to avoid this result it is essential for declarer to cash his Diamond trick promptly; by so doing he follows an important rule, which is that when a cross ruff game is attempted tricks in side suits should be cashed as soon as possible.

Trick 6: North leads a Diamond, and South's King loses to West's Ace.

Trick 7: West leads a trump which is won by South.

This defence is as good as anything that West can do now.

Trick 8: South leads a Diamond to North's Queen.

The difference between the present line of play and the incorrect line described above is that West has to follow to this Diamond lead. He has had no opportunity to throw a Diamond on the fourth round of Spades.

There are now five cards left and declarer is bound to make the remaining tricks by cross-ruffing; he has three trumps and two Spades in his own hand and two trumps in dummy to look after the Spades.

As the reader has quite probably noticed, a better defence by West could have made this contract quite impossible for the declarer. The presence of a singleton Spade in dummy should have warned the defenders to lead trumps in order to prevent Spade ruffs. West should really have led a trump at trick 2, but the game could still have been saved had he done so at trick 3. If a trump is led at the third trick South can, it is true, contrive to ruff three Spades, re-entering his hand twice by means of Club ruffs, but the difficulty will remain that the Diamond trick has not been cleared, and when West wins with the Ace of Diamonds the fifth Club will be fatal to declarer. If after the trump lead at trick 3

South attempts to clear his Diamond trick sooner, West will win and play a second round of trumps, preventing South from ever ruffing more than two Spades.

RETAINING CONTROL OF TRUMPS

In the two examples given so far, declarer has refrained from drawing trumps immediately, once to obtain a discard and once to play a cross ruff. In the next hand we shall find declarer drawing trumps up to a certain point. When there is one master trump against him he will not force it out.

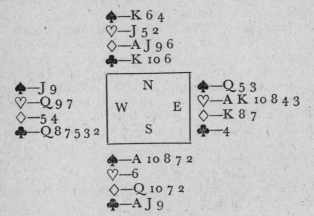

The bidding goes as follows:

South	West	North	East
One Spade.	No.	Two Diamonds.	Two Hearts.
Three Diamonds.	No.	Three Spades.	No.
Four Spades.			

South has bid aggressively, but although short of high cards he has good intermediates (Jacks, 10's, and 9's), and experience has shown that the 5 4 3 1 distribution is powerful for suit play.

Trick 1: West leads ♡ Q, North plays ♡ 2, East plays ♡ 10, South plays ♡ 6.

Trick 2 : West leads ♡ 9, North plays ♡ 5, East plays ♡ K, South trumps ♠ 2.

Trick 3 : South leads ♠ 7, West plays ♠ 9, North plays ♠ K, East plays ♠ 3.

Declarer has no reason to delay trump leads.

Trick 4 : North leads ♠ 4, East plays ♠ 5, South plays ♠ A, West plays ♠ J.

If declarer's trumps had not already been shortened, it would have been good play to finesse the Ten of Spades, a safety play to take care of the possibility that East had all the outstanding trumps. But as things are declarer cannot afford to risk allowing West to win with the Queen or Jack. He must gamble on a 3-2 break of trumps.

This is the critical point in the hand. There is a master trump out against him, and it would be a fatal mistake for declarer to draw it. If he does, another Heart will be led, forcing the last trump, then after the loss of the Diamond finesse East will make three Heart tricks.

Trick 5: South leads ◇ Q, West plays ◇ 4, North plays ◇ 6, East plays ◇ K.

Trick 6: East leads ♠ Q, South plays ♠ 8, West plays ♠ 2, North plays ♠ 6.

It is almost always good play for a defender to play his master trump.

Trick 7: East leads ♡ Ace, South trumps with ♠ 10, West plays ♡ 7, North plays ♡ Jack.

Tricks 8–10 : Declarer makes three tricks in Diamonds.

Declarer now has left A J 9 of Clubs in his own hand, and K 10 6 in dummy. He can finesse for the Queen against either opponent. The decision is far from being a mere guess. It is reached by simple card reading, the process which in more advanced forms is the very essence of expert play. East has been seen to follow to three rounds of trumps and three rounds of Diamonds. Had he five Hearts (remember he bid Two Hearts) and two Clubs, or six Hearts and one Club? The best clue is West's original lead of the Queen of Hearts. Had West had four Hearts, his proper lead would have been his fourth best. Furthermore, if he had had four Hearts to the Queen and two doubletons West might well have raised to three Hearts on the second round of bidding. So the conclusion is that in all probability East had six Hearts and only one Club. Therefore declarer plays the Ace of Clubs and follows with the finesse against West.

The next hand is another example of how carefully declarer must consider the question of drawing trumps.

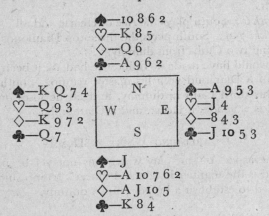

♠—10 8 6 2
♡—K 8 5
◇—Q 6
♣—A 9 6 2

♠—K Q 7 4
♡—Q 9 3
◇—K 9 7 2
♣—Q 7

N W E S

♠—A 9 5 3
♡—J 4
◇—8 4 3
♣—J 10 5 3

♠—J
♡—A 10 7 6 2
◇—A J 10 5
♣—K 8 4

West has no very attractive lead against Four Hearts. The King of Spades is the most likely choice.

Trick 1: West leads ♠ K, North plays ♠ 2, East plays ♠ 5, South plays ♠ J.

Trick 2 : West leads ♠ 4, North plays ♠ 6, East plays ♠ 9, South trumps with ♡ 2.

East can finesse the 9 because it is clear from the lead that his partner holds the Queen.

Now if declarer plays the Ace followed by the King of Hearts he can be defeated. Only one round of Hearts can be taken. South plans to make use of dummy's third trump, and he must not give the opposition a chance to draw it.

Trick 3 : South leads ♡ 6, West plays ♡ 3, North plays ♡ K, East plays ♡ 4.

Trick 4: North leads ◇ Q, East plays ◇ 3, South plays ◇ 5, West plays ◇ K.

Had two rounds of Hearts already been played, West would now cash the Queen, and declarer would inevitably lose a trick in Clubs. As things are, West cannot do better than continue Spades.

Trick 5 : West leads a Spade which is trumped by South.

Trick 6 : South plays the Ace of Hearts and all follow.

Tricks 7–9 : South plays the three top Diamonds, discarding two Clubs from dummy.

It would have made no difference had West been able to ruff a Diamond with his master trump. South can ruff his third Club in dummy, and all he loses on the hand is a Spade, a Heart, and a Diamond.

Establishing a Suit in Dummy

One aspect of suit play which has not yet been discussed is the manner in which declarer's trump suit can be used to establish a broken suit in dummy.

The bidding goes as follows:

South	*North.*
One Spade.	Three Diamonds.
Three Spades.	Four Spades.
Six Spades.	

North would not be wrong to bid only two Diamonds on first round. South is fully justified in bidding a slam.

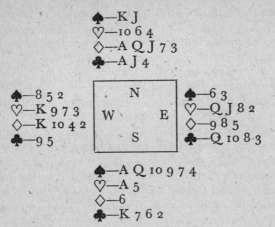

♠—K J
♡—10 6 4
◇—A Q J 7 3
♣—A J 4

♠—8 5 2
♡—K 9 7 3
◇—K 10 4 2
♣—9 5

N
W   E
S

♠—6 3
♡—Q J 8 2
◇—9 8 5
♣—Q 10 8 3

♠—A Q 10 9 7 4
♡—A 5
◇—6
♣—K 7 6 2

His 6-4-2-1 distribution and first- or second-round control in every suit make his hand very powerful.

West has a number of possible leads against Six Spades. On the whole it is good policy to make an attacking lead against a small-slam call, and the best lead therefore is a Heart. West should aim at setting up a trick in Hearts before declarer has established the Diamond suit bid by dummy.

Trick 1 :. West leads ♡ 3, North plays ♡ 4, East plays ♡ J, South plays ♡ A.

Remember that while the top of a sequence is *led*, the lowest card is *played*. When East's Jack of Hearts falls to the Ace, it is clear to West that his partner holds the Queen.

Declarer's plan on this hand should be to establish tricks in Diamonds. He must not draw trumps immediately, because dummy's trumps will be needed as entries for Diamond leads.

Trick 2 : South leads ◇ 6, West plays ◇ 2, North plays ◇ A, East plays ◇ 5.

Although it would not be fatal as the cards lie, it would

be bad play for South to finesse the Jack of Diamonds. If the finesse went wrong, a Heart would be played and the contract would be defeated immediately. By playing the Ace of Diamonds and following with the Queen declarer retains a good chance of making the contract whoever has the King of Diamonds.

Trick 3 : North leads ♦ Q, East plays ♦ 8, South discards ♡ 5, West plays ♦ K.

Had East covered the Queen of Diamonds with the King, South would have trumped, entered dummy with a Spade, led a small Diamond and trumped it, drawn all the trumps, and obtained two discards on the Jack of Diamonds and the fifth Diamond. Since the Queen of Diamonds is not covered the proper play is to discard the losing Heart.

Trick 4 : West leads ♡ 7, North plays ♡ 6, East plays ♡ Q, South trumps with ♠ 4.

Since he knew that his partner held the Queen of Hearts, it was open to West to lead either the King of Hearts or a small one. A good player would lead the small Heart for the rather subtle reason that by retaining the King himself he relieves partner of any necessity to hold on to the Queen of Hearts to prevent dummy's Ten of Hearts from winning. To keep the Queen of Hearts might, in certain circumstances, be awkward for East if he had strength in Clubs.

Trick 5 : South leads ♠ 7, West plays ♠ 2, North plays ♠ J, East plays ♠ 3.

Trick 6 : North leads ♠ K, East plays ♠ 6, South plays ♠ 9, West plays ♠ 5.

Trick 7 : North leads ♦ 3, East plays ♦ 9, South trumps ♠ 10, West plays ♦ 4.

Declarer's plan is to establish the fifth Diamond in dummy as a master. He knows that this can be done if the distribution against him is 4-3. If it is 5-2 and the long Diamond cannot be set up, he will have to resort to the Club finesse. When both oppponents follow to this third round of Diamonds, South knows that he is home.

Trick 8 : South leads ♠ A , West plays ♠ 8, North plays ♡ 10, East plays ♡ 2.

Having drawn this last trump South can enter dummy with the Ace of Clubs and throw two Clubs on the Jack and 7 of Diamonds. So the contract is fulfilled for the loss of one trick in Diamonds.

Declarer exploited the Diamond suit in preference to taking an early finesse in Clubs, because he recognised that a 4-3 division of the outstanding Diamonds would permit him to establish a long-card winner. Calculation of a similar kind occurs in the play of almost every hand and should be instinctive. Our advice to a player wishing to acquire a sense of distribution is, paradoxical as it may seem, never to *count* the various suits; he should *observe* the fall of the cards and with the unchanging suit distributions (4-3-3-3, 4-4-3-2, 5-4-3-1, etc.) always in mind trust his instinct to know when a low card is good, even at the risk of making mistakes at first. A player who needs to count each suit as it is played has as little chance of becoming proficient as a typist who cannot type without looking at the keys.

❧

CHAPTER XIV

A NOTE ON THE LAWS

THE full code of laws is by no means easy to memorize, and in this chapter reference is made only to those laws which deal with the commonest incidents. It should be mentioned in advance that the etiquette of the game demands that penalties for infringements of correct procedure should always be claimed and paid without question, even when the offending side appears to gain no advantage from the misdemeanour.

The Deal

(1) There must be a new deal by the same player if any card is exposed.

(2) By law there should be a new deal if a player looks at a card dealt to him before the deal has been completed. In practice this law is seldom applied but it is nevertheless improper to pick up cards during the deal.

The Auction Period

Improper Calls.

(1) *Misnomers.*—A player may correct a genuine misnomer without penalty.

(2) *Improper Call Condoned.*—An improper call is condoned if the next player bids before attention has been drawn to the irregularity. Suppose, for example, that South bids Two Spades and West makes an insufficient bid of Two Hearts. If before any comment has been made North bids, say, Three Clubs, West's improper call is condoned and the bidding proceeds from Three Clubs.

(3) *Insufficient Bid.*—A player who has made an insufficient bid must, if attention is drawn to the offence before the next opponent has called, make the bid sufficient in the same or in any other denomination. If he makes the bid sufficient by making the lowest sufficient bid in the same denomination if to overcall Two Spades, for example, he amends Two Hearts to Three Hearts, the penalty is that the offender's partner must pass for one round. If the offender makes his bid sufficient in any other way, as by doubling, or by calling another suit, partner must pass throughout.

(4) *Call Out of Turn.*—Unless condoned (as provided in paragraph (2) above), a call out of turn is cancelled and the auction reverts to the player whose turn it was to call. If the call out of turn was a Pass made before

any positive bid had been made, the offender must pass again on the first round. In all other circumstances the offender's partner must pass throughout. The offender is not obliged to repeat his bid and can call as he pleases.

(5) *Illegal Bid.*—The penalty for an impossible bid, such as a double of partner's bid, or a redouble of a call which has not been doubled, or any bid made when the player is obliged by law to pass, is that the offending side must pass throughout, and the opponent who first bid the denomination last bid by his side, or, if neither opponent has bid, the opponent on the offender's left, may cancel the illegal bid.

Card Exposed during the Auction

If one card of less than honour rank is exposed and the owner becomes the defender, the declarer may either prohibit the lead in the suit of such card, or treat it as a penalty card. A penalty card must be left face upwards on the table, and must be played or led at the first opportunity, subject to the obligation to follow suit whenever possible.

If a card of honour rank or more than one card is exposed, there is an additional penalty that the offender's partner must pass throughout the bidding.

THE PLAYING PERIOD

(1) *Reviewing the Bidding.*

Until the opening lead has been made, a player may ask to have all the bidding reviewed. After the lead, the player may ask only what is the contract, and whether, but not by whom, it is doubled or redoubled.

(2) *Lead out of Turn.*

(*a*) A lead out of turn is condoned if the opponent plays to it.

(*b*) If declarer leads from the wrong hand, either

defender may require him to lead from the correct hand, and declarer must, if he can, lead a card of the same suit from the correct hand. For example, if when the lead is in his own hand declarer leads a Spade from dummy, he must when corrected lead a Spade from his own hand. If he fails to do so when not void of Spades, he commits a revoke.

(c) If a defender leads out of turn, declarer may either treat the card led out of turn as a penalty card, or call for the lead of a specified suit from the opponent whose proper turn it is to lead.

(3) *Premature Play by Defender*.

If a defender plays to a trick when it is his partner's turn to play, declarer may require the other defender to play his highest or his lowest card in the suit led, and should he be unable to follow suit, to play a specified suit. Declarer cannot claim any penalty, however, if he has played from both hands himself, not waiting for the defender to play whose proper turn it is. A similar penalty applies if a defender leads to the next trick before his partner has played to the current trick.

(4) *Corrected Revoke*.

If a player fails to follow suit when he can do so, he commits a revoke. If the mistake is discovered in time, the revoke can be corrected. If the revoke is corrected and has been made by (a) a defender, declarer may treat it as a penalty card, or require him to play his highest or lowest card of the correct suit, or (b) the declarer, it may be taken up, and if the defender on declarer's left has played to the trick after declarer, he may require declarer to play his highest or lowest correct card, or (c) dummy, there is no penalty for a revoke. A card played by a player of the non-offending side after a revoke and before its correction may be taken back.

(5) *Established Revoke.*

A revoke, other than one made in leading, becomes established when the offending side leads or plays to the next trick, except that such a revoke made on the twelfth trick never becomes established. A revoke made in leading becomes established when the offender's partner plays to the revoke trick. When a revoke has been established, the trick stands as played, and if the revoke is claimed, tricks won in play by the revoking side after its first revoke (including the revoke trick) are transferred to the non-offending side at the end of play—two such tricks for a side's first revoke, and one such trick for every subsequent revoke by the same side. There is no penalty for a revoke by dummy. It is important to note the provision that only tricks made from the time of the revoke can be transferred.

(6) *Hands not Played Out.*

If declarer claims or concedes one or more of the remaining tricks he must leave his hand face upwards on the table, and either opponent may require him to play on, or to make a statement of how he intends to play the remaining tricks. A very important rule is that declarer may not take any finesse which is not announced at the time of such claim or concession. If a side concedes a trick which it could not lose by any play of the cards, such a concession is void.

(7) *Dummy's Rights.*

Dummy forfeits all his rights if he intentionally looks at the face of a card in a player's hand. Subject to this provision, dummy is allowed to reply to a player's proper question, discuss questions of fact or law, question declarer regarding his possible revoke, draw attention to a defender's irregularity (such as a lead out of turn or a revoke) and ask declarer whether he knows his rights.

If after overlooking another player's hand dummy draws attention to an irregularity, no penalty can be claimed; nor can any penalty be claimed if dummy exceeds his rights by suggesting a particular penalty, instead of merely stating the law.

(8) *Penalty Card of a Defender.*

If during the play a defender drops a card face upwards on the table, sees the face of any of his partner's cards, makes a remark which discloses any of his cards to his partner, or names any card in his partner's hand, such card becomes a penalty card. A penalty card must be left face up on the table until played, and whenever it is the turn of the defender who owns it to play—subject to his duty to follow suit—he must play it. If he has two or more penalty cards, declarer may require him to play any one of them. There is no penalty if declarer exposes a card, since he gains no advantage by doing so.